Published by 404 Ink Limited
www.404Ink.com
@404Ink

Editing: Heather McDaid
Proofreading & typesetting: Laura Jones
Cover design: Luke Bird
Co-founders and publishers of 404 Ink:
Heather McDaid & Laura Jones

Print ISBN: 978-1-912489-72-5
Ebook ISBN: 978-1-912489-73-2

Printed and bound in Great Britain by Clays Ltd, Elcograf S.p.A.

BFFs

The Radical Potential of Female Friendship

Anahit Behrooz

Inklings

Contents

For Michelle Hulford,
who set the standard

'One sister have I in our house,
And one, a hedge away'
– Emily Dickinson

'So much has been left out, unattempted.'
– A Room of One's Own, **Virginia Woolf**

Spoilers

Extensive plot points and spoilers are revealed in the discussions on the following texts. Proceed with caution!

Chapter 1
Sula, Toni Morrison (1973)
The Neopolitan Novels, Elena Ferrante (2012-2015)
Booksmart, dir. Olivia Wilde (2019)

Chapter 2
The Virgin Suicides, Jeffrey Eugenides (1993)
The Virgin Suicides, dir. Sofia Coppola (1999)

Chapter 3
Grey's Anatomy, created by Shonda Rimes (2005-present)
Insecure, created by Issa Rae and Larry Wilmore (2016-2021)
Betty, created by Crystal Moselle (2020-2021)

Chapter 4
Animals, Emma Jane Unsworth (2014)
Frances Ha, dir. Noah Baumbach (2012)
Girlfriends, dir. Claudia Weill (1978)
Fiona and Jane, Jean Chen Ho (2022)

Content notes

The following themes are discussed in *BFF*s:

Sexual and gendered violence:
Girlhood, p14
Push, p16
Sula, p19-20
Neopolitan novels, p25
Thelma and Louise, p59-60
9 to 5, p60
Reading Lolita in Tehran, p64

Suicide:
Werther, p16
The Virgin Suicides, p45-49

Racism and racial violence:
Sula, p18-19

Abortion and reproductive rights:
Dirty Dancing, p40-41
Grey's Anatomy, p52
Girlfriends, p80

Introduction

In the Middle Ages, in the supposed dark ages of European civilisation, a woman wrote a book about a city made up only of women. *The Book of the City of Ladies* follows author Christine de Pizan as she builds a city trench by trench and stone by stone, scrabbling in the earth to carve out walls and dwelling spaces for its future inhabitants, accompanied by three Virtues who extol womankind's moral, social, and intellectual value. de Pizan wrote the book as a response to centuries of male commentariat about women and it is in many ways an act of revisionist solidarity: as the likes of Mary Magdalene, Sappho, Esther and Saint Cecilia weave in and out of the pages, the fictionalised de Pizan confronts the misogynist narratives that have long structured her own perception of her gender. 'For you know that any evil spoken of women so generally only hurts those who say it,' de Pizan concludes, 'not women themselves.'[1]

de Pizan was one of the first women to write this kind of all-female utopia, but it is a genre that has recurred again and again in the centuries that have followed. Charlotte Perkins Gilman, best known for her eerie Gothic tale 'The Yellow Wallpaper' about a woman driven insane by marital domination, is also known for her serialised novel *Herland*, in which a society made up of asexually-reproducing women is characterised by total peace and freedom from power. When a group of male explorers stumble across this hidden-away society, their singular masculine presence throws into relief the emancipation of *Herland*'s women from rigid gender roles, and the radical, non-hierarchical forms of relation and childrearing that are allowed to flourish instead. A year before *Herland* was published, meanwhile, Bengal feminist, activist, and education advocate Begum Rokeya wrote 'Sultana's Dream', a speculative short story set in Ladyland, where women run a peaceful, thriving society in which men are shut away in male purdahs.

None of these stories are about female friendship, strictly conceived, yet within each of them – from the medieval proto-feminist treatise of de Pizan to the Bengali satire of Rokeya – lies an imagination for a different kind of world, one of community, solidarity, and mutual understanding that extends far beyond the trappings of patriarchal power. The conditions of these literary utopias are defined not just as a place where men aren't, but as a place where the patriarchal structures that have long confined female intimacy are fiercely refused. In *Herland*, there is no marriage, and motherhood has become a community endeavour, carried out in partnership with other women who share burdens of care, education, and safeguarding. In the similarly named Ladyland in 'Sultana's Dream', the narrator – long used to meeting her friend in the private confines of the Botanic Gardens away from men – is both terrified and elated at being able to enact their friendship in the public commons, at the sudden liberty this signifies.

I have always been unlucky in romance, and lucky in friendship. I almost wrote 'unlucky in love', but this is not true; yet the instinct exists – to pour all our experience of love into one particular vessel. My friendships have been vast, encompassing, and structuring, framing all the important and unimportant moments in my life. There have been friends at parties and as neighbours and in hospitals and running errands and holding my hand, screaming off the edge of a sharp cliff. I don't really think of them as family, because this implies that family is the only way to practise such strong bonds of care. They are just, in every way, crucial to my life: to the everyday and the grand future and everything in between.

They are also something that I wanted very badly, even in the extreme shyness of my childhood. There was probably an element of idealism in that desire – I grew up on the boarding school novels of British children's literature, and I just desperately wanted to belong. But I think I understood, even in that distracted childhood state where everything is taken at face value, that there was something vital in expanding where we find intimacy and community. There is, here, a line from the Hugh Grant comedy *About A Boy* that I return to often. In it, a small Nicholas Hoult looks around at his tiny traditional family, his mentally unwell mother and his complete lack of support systems and has a revelation. 'That's when I realised: two people isn't enough,' he says. 'You've got to have backup. If there are only two people, and one of you drops off the edge, you're on your own.' There were, granted, more than two of us in my very loving family, but there still existed an always looming potential for isolation – we were a small, first-generation family, had very few relatives nearby, and no community beyond ourselves. I understood this need for backup, the security it represented but also the richness; bright new threads pulled through an existing tapestry.

Yet as I have aged and as these backups have passed through the charm of youthful friendship, their security in my life has become increasingly fraught. We have a tendency in our society to assign female friendships to childhood, and once we are past that point, there exist very few public structures in which to contain or mediate them. As critical theorist Lauren Berlant explains:

'Desires for intimacy that bypass the couple or the life narrative it generates have no alternative plots, let alone few laws and stable spaces of culture in which to clarify and to cultivate them. What happens to the energy of attachment when it has no designated space? To the glances, gestures, encounters, collaborations, or fantasies that have no canon?'[2]

Love and attachment need *somewhere to go*, people to be poured into, a home to spread out and thrive. I think of Fleabag, heartbroken after her mother's funeral.

'I don't know what to do with it,' she sobs. 'With all the love I have for her. I don't know where to put it now.'

'I'll take it,' her best friend tells her.

We need a wealth of people to absorb the sheer depths of our desires, and fixed spaces of culture to understand these intimacies. When these spaces are limited to only one kind of narrative, the people who live their lives according to other intimacies can become, as Berlant argues, 'unimaginable, even often to themselves.'[3]

Female intimacy has always been bound up in the patriarchy, and in particular the heteronormative, monogamous structures of relation that have kept the patriarchy afloat, tying women's interior and intimate lives to the entrenchment of male social, financial, and legal power. The horrifying chattel roots of marriage, in which women were passed between families to solidify political and economic contracts, are well known; yet marriage and the nuclear family – even in our ostensible golden age of modernity where women can keep their surnames and governments can still force them into childbirth and domesticity – continue to act in the service of maintaining patriarchal and capitalist forms of power. There is, even to my own ears, something cynical about this claim, but this is perhaps the point: the careful rehabilitation of marriage and the nuclear family in the past century has worked hard to obfuscate their continued use as tools of power.

As Tom Rasmussen explains in *First Comes Love: On Marriage and Other Ways of Being Together*, '[m]arriage remains a tool of the state: a way of keeping society in recognisable shape.'[4] Marriage, monogamy, and the nuclear family, Rasmussen argues, have become, at least in Western society, an abdication of responsibility on the part of the government to care for its citizens; an extension in many ways of the slow decay of the welfare state; 'a system that demands we prioritise one another so that the state doesn't have to prioritise us.'[5] The stress placed on marriage and the nuclear family, from the dominance of heterosexual stories on screen to the absence of safe and diverse sex education, is largely a means of ensuring free childcare, healthcare, and elder care from individuals in society, typically women. Romantic relationships should not necessarily rely on doing away with other forms of intimacy but, in a society where women continue to be seen as potential sources of free and unlimited domestic labour, they do. Keeping female intimacy tied to these structures is profoundly necessary for the maintenance of the patriarchal capitalist state and, by the same stroke, liberating it is profoundly radical.

How can we have a more expansive understanding of female intimacy and interiority – our capacities for community and desire and disappointment and attachment – if we resist the patriarchal modes of relation through which these have always been mediated? What kind of connections and systems of care might be allowed to thrive? How can we represent our interior lives with the depth and complexity they contain, and in doing so, see ourselves anew?

I think of Berlant, about what can be made imaginable, when my two best friends and I pass amongst each other, like furtive digital contraband, a viral AITA (Am I the Asshole?) Reddit post about three friends who live on neighbouring farms, with dogs and goats and chickens running between their enclosures. In this post, one of the women frets about her other friends' outraged responses when she prioritises the ones she lives with. 'If she's expected to put her husband first before her friends,' she asks, 'then what's wrong with me saying I need to put my friends who I essentially live with and share most of my life with?'⁶ Underlying her frustration is a crucial point about the types of relationships we are allowed to centralise; within it is also a glimpse of something now imaginable that my friends and I whisper to each other whenever we are sad, lonely, tired, or miss each other.

'Just think of the chickens,' we tell each other, a strange shibboleth of our yearning for attachment and togetherness. 'One day that'll be us.' It likely won't be, but there is a language of precedence now for the entanglement of our lives.

Culture is important: it allows us to see what is possible. From the erratic public commons of social media, supposedly democratising all walks of life, to the films, books, and television that fill our leisure time, culture and the arts expand our horizons of feasibility, giving us glimpses into other lives that might be ours, if we allowed them to be. Experiences of non-romantic, non-sexual or non-familial intimacy have very few stable spaces against which to define themselves. There exists practically no legal or economic framework through which friendship is codified in our society: your best friend, however in love you are, cannot obtain a residency visa through you; you cannot claim tax breaks together; and there will be no grand celebrations to mark the declaration and milestones of your relationship. It is in art – even amidst the normative representations that continue to overwhelm the canon – that such spaces of alternative intimacy can be carved out, recognised and legitimised. Friendships can become everything. The meet-cute, the drama, the heartbreak. The love story. The whole plot.

Such friendship is, of course, a broad church; so much is held under its eaves. 'A best friend isn't a person, Danny,' Mindy Lahiri exasperatedly informs her co-worker in *The Mindy Project*, 'it's a tier.' We have, in our culture, a real lack of vocabulary to describe these kinds of ties, fierce and intricate and binding, an absence of language for the determined, capillary ways they wind through our histories and our lives. Much of what follows in *BFFs* mirrors typical structures of romance – from whirlwind affairs to bruised break-ups – because these friendships, platonic though they are, are also romantic. I think of my friends: hands tangled in hair, lives lived in tandem, the first port in any storm. Understanding these relationships in all their passion, friction, and tenderness is less to insist on the totalisation of romantic intimacy in all modes of relation, but rather to liberate the narrative of romance from its heteronormative, monogamous remits. Relationships that are platonic, but also romantic. Not queer, but queered.

This book looks at female friendships as a site of radical intimacy, as told by the literature, cinema, and television that form canons of alternative attachment. My focus on solely female friendships arises not out of a smug idea that only women are capable of such depths of attachment, nor out of a desire to enclose and define the boundaries of female experience. I write about female intimacy because it is what I know, but there absolutely exists a book about representations of male friendship (just think of *The Great Escape*, *Scrubs*, or *Matthias + Maxime*). Masculinity and male intimacy are complex and inherently gendered modes of behaviour, forged as much in the crucible of patriarchal suffocation as female interiority, and with as much to signal about the permitted attachments that structure our communal and intimate lives. In the same way, a book absolutely exists on the specificities of trans, nonbinary and gender fluid communities, and indeed this book owes much – if not everything – to the histories of queer radical thought that precede it, to the long and hard work these have done in joyfully expanding our conceptualisations of connection and community. Here, my definition of 'female', such as it is, is left deliberately broad, encompassing all those who have some experience of socialised femininity or who see within the worlds of the following chapters some kind of correlation to their own lives.

'Satisfying friendships in which we share mutual love provide a guide for behaviour in other relation-ships, including romantic ones,' bell hooks writes. 'They provide us all with a way to know community.'[7] I first heard this some months ago, read out loud by my best friend. She is curled up in bed next to me, weeks into a months-long stay. She knows I am due to write this book, and knows I will perhaps find this useful. She was, of course, right. The weight of our collective lives settles between us, and is somehow shared. It is impossible to tease out the threads of my life from those I have lived it with; the knot sits there, a joyful tangle of wanting to love big and wide and more. At its heart, this book is dedicated to that idea of more. To the sisterhoods that form us, the rifts that break our hearts, the communities we create. As our conceptualisations of the nuclear family and female intimacy begin to shift and morph into something more expansive, we have become, in a way, the new romantics of the stories we tell. But I know – as I look around at my life and the people around me, at the playgrounds and the flat shares and every moment in between – that we were also the first.

Chapter 1
Coming-of-age

There are three girls, and they are dancing. The light of the motel room is inky dim; there is no sound, just a song played sharp and bright over their movements. Their smiles are enchanted, arms and fingers interlocked, every gesture both carefree and bursting with affection. From the bed, another girl watches, her face beatific. She scrambles up and then there are four girls, tangled and in love. Their voices suddenly join the song, an unruly joy echoing against its polish. Rihanna's 'Diamonds' fills the air, and it feels like it could have been written about them.

In Céline Sciamma's 2014 coming-of-age film *Girlhood*, the setting of the Parisian banlieues – long a distinctly masculine space through cultural landmarks such as Mathieu Kassovitz's gritty 1995 film *La Haine*, which gave voice to the disenfranchisement of France's urban communities – is transfigured through the story of a young girl who falls in with a new crowd. They walk around malls, hold amateur fight clubs, and navigate the combined violence of adolescence and their milieux; yet amidst the heartbreak of their lives – neglected by the state, abandoned by the education system, and bearing the immediate anger of the men around them – there is one indelible image that stands firm and vivid, that I return to again and again. These girls, blue-black in the burgeoning dawn, entwined and together. Released in the original French as *Bande de Filles*, meaning 'group of girls' or girl gang, the film became, in the Anglo-speaking world, *Girlhood*; but I am not sure all that much changed in that blunt exchange of words. There is a time in our lives, after all, when they mean practically the same thing.

What is this unwavering entanglement between childhood and friendship? It is, in some ways, a strange state of affairs – our immediate connotation of one for the other. The friendships we form in adulthood can in practicality be stronger, longer-lasting, more representative of the people we have become and will continue to be. Yet we are, culturally, fascinated by the childhood and adolescent friendship, by the bonds of girlhood that turn us, in so many ways, into who we are. *Anne of Green Gables*, *Mallory Towers*, *Lady Bird*, *The Color Purple*, *Clueless*, *The Craft*, *Mean Girls*… the list is endless, climbing far higher than representations of female friendship in later life. Perhaps it is because they occur at the crucial point when we are slowly coagulating into who we become; perhaps it is because they occupy that pre-marriageable age when they are still allowed to be our primary relationships. Girlhood. Girl gang. The boundaries between the words bend and bow, until they barely exist at all.

'How do we know who we are, if not in relation?' Nancy K. Miller asks in her friendship memoir *My Brilliant Friends*.[1] Yet the inherently collective nature of identity formation has not always been so well understood. Despite its contemporary association with female friendship, the coming-of-age story was historically situated in a distinctly individualist tradition, interested in the ways in which male authority and independence are forged within dominant social structures. The genre traces back to the Bildungsroman, or the novel of education, a new genre of writing that began with Goethe's eighteenth-century German novel *The Sorrows of Young Werther* and continued in the likes of Charles Dickens' 1861 classic *Great Expectations*, Rudyard Kipling's 1901 adventure tale *Kim* and Jack London's 1909 class critique *Martin Eden*. Formed in the emerging modernity of the Enlightenment and Romanticism, with their fascination with individual genius and the supposedly emancipatory possibilities of teleological growth, the traditional, masculine Bildungsroman held as its ideals a sense of the

15

self that was isolated, an identity that had to be carved out on one's own. The endeavour was not always successful (is there any better indictment of the genre's focus on the individual than the suicide of its first protagonist, the idealistic and entirely unequipped Werther?) but the narrative structure, and purpose, persisted.

It is difficult to say exactly when this began to shift – when the genre began to consider how gender might skew this juggernaut-like trajectory towards an individually realised self. Some credit Jane Austen with the first female coming-of-age tales, but her novels are really marriage plots, concerned with the economic determining contexts of women's intimate lives. Certainly, by the time Louisa May Alcott wrote *Little Women*, the genre was beginning to expand, and in doing so, began to understand the deceptive parameters of individualism that the traditional coming-of-age story set up. What does the Bildungsroman, the so-called novel of education mean, when Jo March is forced to wave a grudging Laurie off to university, herself aching to attend? How do its bourgeois aspirations translate in the poverty-tinged existence in Sandra Cisneros's 1984 novel *The House on Mango Street,* about a Chicana girl in a deprived Chicago neighbourhood? What is it to come of age when your very childhood is denied, as with Precious in Sapphire's exploration of sexual trauma in the 1996 novel *Push?*

There is a wayward delight in watching a genre burst at its seams, become expansive and disorderly and all-encompassing. The increasingly gendered and inter-sectional concerns of the coming-of-age story allow us to see not only the emotional and psychological matu-ration of previously ignored protagonists, but the social and political conditions which inform their lives. And the social and political is always, always collective. As in Sciamma's *Girlhood*, the rich archive of this kind of tale is dense not only with individual identity formation, but with the interdependence of the group, with the ways in which we come of age together. Childhood, these stories understand, is a wonderfully and frighteningly porous thing. We are raised as much by our friends – the small, equally unformed beings scattered around us – as we are by our parents and guardians: taught at their bloody, gingham-ed knees not just who we want to be, but how we want to be loved.

Miles away from the strict education novels of the late-eighteenth century, the long history of the female coming-of-age story pulls at the tension between the indi-vidual and the communal, navigating the strange chaos of growing selfhood alongside our capacity for headlong, pluralising intimacy. Contained within these friendships is something intense and precarious that subverts the supposed idyll of childhood: all the untapped desires of our inchoate selves meeting the demands of increasingly rigid assemblies of femininity. The bonds of our girlhoods, I believe, can be romantic but they are not *romantic*. Rather, there is something discomforting about their fierceness, their hypersensitivity, their lack of abandon. Liquid bright and malleable, we form ourselves within our cohorts, both alone and together. As we come of age, so do our friendships, their intimacies pulled in the bruised wake of adolescent anguish. There is so much potential for loveliness here. There is so much potential for shatter.

Toni Morrison's *Sula* is a book about such friendship, its knitted beauty and unnerving brutality. The events of the novel are set in a small Black neighbourhood in the uplands of Ohio in the 1920s and '30s, and the narrative takes its time to get to the eponymous Sula and her strange, feverish sisterhood with Nel, the quiet, obedient girl she befriends in their youth. Rather, the first third tells the history of their community: the Bottom, a wooded, hilled area 'gifted' by a slave owner to a previously enslaved man whom he tricks into accepting the agriculturally inferior land. This exercise of malicious white power lays the groundwork for everything: the poverty that dogs Sula and Nel's childhoods, the violence that scaffolds their intrepid attachment. Tender and impetuous though it may be, their friendship is never quite allowed innocence, not really, too embroiled as it is in the hostility of its surroundings. Early on, when four white boys torment Nel on her way home from school,

Sula wordlessly pulls out a paring knife and slices off the tip of her finger. 'If I can do that to myself,' she asks them, 'what you suppose I'll do to you?'[2] Blood may be thicker than water, but Sula and Nel's friendship becomes evidence of the long-forgotten fullness of this axiom: the blood of the covenant is thicker than the water of the womb, the ties that we choose stronger than the ones we are born into.

In the slow drip-drip of her blood, in the tiny scrap of flesh left on the road, Sula renders her very self open and permeable to the muddle of her and Nel's girlish connection. Images of such porosity wind throughout: Sula and Nel silently lying against each other in the grass, each unconsciously copying the other in gestures and play; Sula and Nel walking in tandem past a crowd of men in the multiplied burgeoning of their sexuality; Sula recalling in adulthood 'the days when we were two throats and one eye and we had no price.'[3] On the cover of my copy – a 1980 edition bound in plastic from the public library – two little girls appear silhouetted, surrounded by a ghostly, or perhaps an angelic, glow. They look practically the same, although not much can be made out except four large eyes and two smock dresses covering gangly limbs. But towards the bottom the dresses begin to merge, blurred into a single garment that holds the girls attached at the waist, the hips, their covered knees; a gradual and willing immersion.

In her reading of *Sula* in *The Paris Review*, Namwali Serpell writes about Morrison's insistence on such instability, about her investigation of the sly potential of girlhood friendship to reconstitute the self. 'I'm feeling this trembling time,' Serpell writes, 'its desire and ache… this girlish queerness – neither straight nor lesbian exactly, but feverish with slant possibility – this dewy conspiracy of selves.'[4] In literature, the theme of the double – materialising as twins and echoes and unlikely sympathies – has long typically signalled a Gothic uncanniness, a signifier of psychological fracture, but here in *Sula* its presence is perversely restorative. Friendship as dewy conspiracy, underground collusion. The strange twinning of Nel and Sula's relationship is eerie not in its fragmentation of the self but in its disobedience of individual selfhood, refusing the placid singularity that these narratives ought to entail. The transgression of their bond disturbs the normativity of their surroundings: together, the girls watch in horror as a child they play with drowns, they feel the undisguised lust of male gazes on their bodies, they replace the lost love of their parents with their own. 'You. Sula. What's the difference?'[5] Nel is asked in adulthood, as they – long past the days of childhood osmosis – collapse together again, and again.

Such stories can reorient our conceptualisations of female intimacy and identity formation, fastening them together so tightly that they become one and the same. But in their focus on the hazardous tipping point of adolescence, they also call attention to the looming demands that can pull such intimacy apart. Adulthood, the spectre that haunts the coming-of-age tale, arrives; in *Sula*, it takes the form of the eponymous protagonist leaving the Bottom to pursue a university education while Nel remains to get married and, most finally, when she returns and sleeps with Nel's husband. Yet Morrison is less interested in Sula's stampeding of the laws of monogamous alliance than in Nel's anger, in her decision to give more value to the broken contract of her marriage than to her and Sula's bond. 'She had clung to Nel as the closest thing to both other and a self,' Morrison writes of Sula, 'only to discover that she and Nel were not one and the same thing.'[6] For Sula, it is not her adultery with Nel's husband but Nel's objection to it which is a betrayal – of their shared collapse of boundaries, of the doubled experience that she believed constituted their friendship.

The concept of the frenemy – the friendship, especially that of adolescence, based in or culminating in jealousy and resentment – recurs repeatedly in the coming-of-age narrative. Its overwhelming presence within our cultural conversation emanates partly from a need to undermine alternative possibilities of female intimacy, to cast doubt on the integrity of women's emotional lives. But there is also a dormant truth to it that we find difficult to admit: a reflection of the people we are, and the contexts we grow up in, than who we wish we were. I find it hard to write about the friendships of youth – I have found it hard to write this chapter – because it is impossible to think about my own friendships from this time without regret: not for their intensity, but for the fraught, often ugly tensions of envy and bitterness that co-existed alongside.

They shaped, in a way, how I came to understand friendship, a behaviour that I have been trying to unlearn ever since: you are drawn, thrillingly, to the most brilliant people, only to find in this brilliance the possibility of your own dimness, your own lack. This is not something I, or I imagine anyone else, is proud of. But it is useless to pretend it doesn't exist. 'Envy has always been my fallback emotion, despite persistent efforts to root it out,' Miller explains, adding later, with an ironic frustration: 'We were feminists, after all. We did not believe in penis envy, and we did not believe in feminine rivalry.'[7] The theory is sound, but the practice – that is another story.

Miller's *My Brilliant Friends*, an account of three fundamental friendships formed in adulthood during the height of feminism's second wave, is explicitly informed by Elena Ferrante's seminal Neapolitan novels: *My Brilliant Friend, The Story of a New Name, Those Who Leave and Those Who Stay*, and *The Story of the Lost Child*. In an article for Prism, Nudrat Kamal describes Ferrante's series as a portrait of 'one of, if not *the* most compelling literary female friendships ever'[8] and in my own life, I notice that everyone I speak to about her novels responds in quiet hesitation, as if dazed by their needlepoint acuity into the fractiousness of female intimacy. It feels almost that, in the shadow of Ferrante's unmasking, we have nothing left to say. What can you say about the sensation of discovering the silences of your own life, its bitten-tongue desires and distorted regrets, pressed between the pages of something so external to you? It is the witchcraft of literature to transgress the boundaries of the self, to cast a spell of unnerving premonition.

Ferrante's tetralogy follows two women – Elena 'Lenù' Greco and Raffaella 'Lila' Cerullo – from childhood through to middle age, and the troubled, uneasy interdependence that structures their lives. Told through Lenù's eyes as she looks back on their friendship after an elderly Lila suddenly disappears, her extended recollection charts their coming-of-age in 1950s Naples, a world of dust-stricken poverty and naturalised violence, and the forces over the decades that pull them apart and draw them back together: Lenù's scholarship to high school and university while the fiercely intelligent Lila does not make it past grade school, their marriages and affairs with intersecting men from the neighbourhood, their shared ambivalences and obsessions of motherhood. Ferrante's narrative is sprawling, evoking the grand realist novels of the nineteenth century, so that it is the friendship between Lenù and Lila that braids its tentacular plot together, that determines and organises the motion of their lives.

I have spoken about the inherent romance of female friendships but it is hard to see anything romantic about Lenù and Lila's relationship, unless it mimics – even in childhood – the rhythms and roils of an old marriage, stained and acrid with disappointment. There are relatively few instances of warm, unfettered intimacy between them, few moments of conspiracy: they speak sharp to one another, respond grudgingly in the face of the other's achievements, and act in all the selfishness of a life of scarce rewards. They, frankly, barely seem to like each other – or, perhaps this is unfair. The book is narrated through Lenù's voice, and Lila's antagonism, her maliciousness and jealousy in the face of Lenù's desire for success, are entirely mediated through Lenù, the world's most unreliable of narrators. I listen to the tetralogy as an audiobook and at times it feels unbearable, as if trapped in the repetition of my own worst thoughts.

Bluntly, each wants what the other has. Lila, poor and dispossessed and entirely replete with ambition and scope, is made to witness her 'brilliant friend', a girl who passes through the milestones of schooling at a time when it was almost impossible. Ferrante's novels, in a way, literalise the origins of the Bildungsroman through a gendered reading of twentieth-century class, where an education is not simply a means of existential self-improvement, but a path out of destitution. For Lenú, however, her charmed Cinderella story means very little in the perceived encroachment of Lila's complex interiority: in the blatant knowledge of her unplumbed intelligence, careless good looks, and singular, enviable determination. Lila is beautiful, desired, marries first at only sixteen, has sex first, never mind that she is brutally raped by her husband on her wedding night. Even her traumas render her more interesting; she is made radiant not despite, but because of her circumstances.

I feel sick with recognition. But I also feel an anxious sympathy for Lenù, wretched though she can be, for she inhabits a political reality from which logic cannot move her. In the desperate world in which they come of age, where drudgery and domestic violence await just around the corner, their friendship is embedded in an inescapable framework of capitalist patriarchy: competition is inevitable and the thoughts, validation, and attention of men hold indispensable value. It is, I often think, so impossible to be a woman in this world, with millennia upon millennia of structural violence eroding away at your life. And yet, I can recall, it can be even more impossible as a child, with the threat of adulthood and womanhood not yet realised or addressed, but hanging low and pregnant in the sky. Here, Ferrante tells us, are the conditions that create the impossibility of alternative intimacies, even in the innocuousness of youth. Such conditions undermine the intoxication of being fused to another's life, they whisper cunningly that, in the eyes of those that matter, somebody else is doing it better.

In her memoir *Little Weirds*, writer and comedian Jenny Slate paints a portrait of femininity that is performed, an extravagant and artificially unconscious spectacle staged for men. She imagines an onlooker lingering in the peripheries of her life, his alchemical gaze materialising the edges of her selfhood. '[H]e sees me pay no mind to anyone but myself as I carry my groceries,' Slate says. 'He sees me being satisfied and self-sufficient. He sees me as myself when nobody is watching, except he is watching.'[9] I remember reading this years ago and, disturbed, sending it to a friend only to be met with her unexpected resistance; she was frustrated by Slate's urgent need for male validation. Yet I am not sure denying the everyday virulence of the male gaze helps us be liberated from it. Increasingly, rather, I feel that our whole lives since childhood are decided in the panopticon of its attention, as if it, rather than our elected intimacies, were the organising principle of our lives.

'Wanted was the only thing I was sure I ought to be,' Melissa Febos writes in her memoir *Girlhood*. 'There it was, bright in the eyes of every boy in that driveway. A reflection of me that bore a different mark.'[10] In Ferrante's novels, life takes place entirely in and through others' gazes; the narrator Lenù's, to be sure, but also the sundry of domineering, conniving, needing men that stare at and desire and discard the girls. Succumbing to this gaze and striving towards the traditional confines of womanhood – that is to say, becoming object rather than subject – is, much like Lenù's education, a path towards economic security for us all. But more than that, it is a tantalising form of social currency. Here is a woman who is wanted, fuckable, made visible in the eyes of the public sphere. Here is a woman who has done her job.

Contained within the eddying hostility and affection of Lila and Lenù's friendship, then, is more than mere jealousy, more than the much-derided female cattiness that the traditional discourse around the frenemy suggests. Both Morrison and Ferrante's novels are, perhaps, so staggering – *the* books on female friendship, no less – because they understand friendship as a political category, one that reflects the broader structures of patriarchy, poverty, and racial violence that determine female intimacy from its earliest days. As with Nel, caught between placing value on her marriage or friendship, Lenù is torn between two worlds: a world of solidarity that has nothing to prove and everything to give, and one which calls for her neatly partitioned identity, her complicity in the roles of femininity and social mobility that are prescribed for her since childhood.

'Become,' Lenù considers. 'It was a verb that had always obsessed me [...] I had wanted to become something – here was the point – only because I was afraid that Lila would become someone and I would stay behind. My becoming was a becoming in her wake.'[11] Throughout the length of Ferrante's narrative, Lenù constantly seeks to disentangle herself from what she sees as the claustrophobia of her and Lila's ensnared becoming. Yet does it really matter if our becoming is in the wake of another? Isn't there something remarkable about being caught in the froth of someone else's life, pulled along by the same ebbing tides? Despite Lenù's frustration with the limpet cling of Lila's subjectivity on her own, their relationship opens up possibilities of intimacy that lie beyond the violence of the patriarchal relations that otherwise determine their lives. Lila and Lenù intellectually pushing each other, raising their children in neighbouring apartments, only having each other – if only they could recognise it.

Best friends forever. The maxim, broken across necklaces and scrawled in exercises books, applies nowhere as much as the coming-of-age friendship, where such promises are so easily and earnestly made, and so often rent apart. Contained within the phrase – its aspirational optimism and latent unreliability, its entanglement with the forces that seek to sever it – lies the tension of female friendship, its simultaneously generative and expiring nature. It is near impossible to write its story without acknowledging this decay, this contradiction. Both

Morrison and Ferrante understood the dark complication of such friendship: the way it pokes and prods and tends to all your softest, most guileless parts; a constant stripping off and binding of an emerging wound.

The kind of friendship that *Sula* and the Neapolitan novels depict, serious and snarled and devastating, sets a standard for a conceptualisation of coming-of-age that both recognises the power of patriarchal forms of identity formation, and thinks beyond its boundaries. For all their distinctly unromantic approach, there is something strangely hopeful about them, holding as they do an imagination of ties whose marks linger even in the determined loosening of the world. This imagination has come to permeate the mainstream of our culture in recent years, in works that transplant female friendship into genres traditionally concerned with romantic relationships. 2018 film *Banana Split* examines the pain of teen heartbreak through the sudden, fervent friendship between two girls who have both dated the same boy. *Never Have I Ever*, a classic will-they-won't-they, love triangle television show spends as much time on its protagonist Devi's imperfect, ardent relationship with her best friends as it does on her various flirtations with boys. Casey McQuiston's young adult novel *I Kissed Shara Wheeler* places narrative importance not just on romance but on the fizz of queer community. Even small-town drama *Gilmore Girls*, whose supposed best-friendship between Rory and Lane is troublingly noxious and uneven, finds strange, prickly magic in the relationship between Rory and Paris as a cipher for ambition and change.

And of course, there is Olivia Wilde's 2019 film *Booksmart*, which felt revolutionary on release for something so simple as making friendship the centre of gravity around which everything else revolves. In it, best friends Molly (Beanie Feldstein) and Amy (Kaitlyn Dever) are inseparable in the sentimental way you can really only be in the fierce myopia of youth. Having spent their entire childhoods together, they are now facing the first proper separation they have known in their young lives and determine to have one (their only) wild night before the end of school. Their journey turns into a kind of adolescent odyssey through the transition from childhood to adulthood – spacey classmates become the Scylla and Charybdis that threaten to derail the quest, an awkward Lyft driver the ferryman as the city of Los Angeles slips past like water beneath the bow. The original script, written in the late noughties by Emily Halpern and Sarah Haskins, centred on two girls trying to find last-minute boyfriends before prom, but under new screenwriters Susanna Fogel, Katie Silberman and director Wilde became more subversive: an exploration of the kind of people Molly and Amy want to become, the experiences – romantic and otherwise – that they long to have, and the navigation of their friendship in the impending reality of adulthood.

Romance still figures – Amy has a crush on skater girl Ryan and Molly has fallen for the head of the popular kids Nick – but these relationships are always framed through the girls' interactions. Molly's giddiness when in Nick's glow is palpable, but the emotional core of her attraction is mediated through her disclosure of it to Amy, and when a girl Amy hooks up with comes to return her underwear, the scene ends with Amy running to tell Molly. The entire dramatic thrust of *Booksmart* is marked in the shifting landscape of their relationship, mimicking the traditional romance of the teen movie – the bonding and the fractures and the make-ups. 'You are the smartest, strongest, coolest, most stunningly gorgeous creature this high school and this earth has ever seen and Nick would be lucky to be a footnote in your story,' Amy tells Molly, and it is John Cusack holding up a hi-fi, Freddie Prinze Jr. at the foot of the stairs, Heath Ledger, boyish smile alight, clutching a guitar in his hands.

The friendship in *Booksmart* is situated in a heart-on-its-sleeve, Generation Z feminist politics that saturates the film; the girls' ambitions and fierce bond are cast in this light, a marked departure from the traditional concerns of teen protagonists who searched for romance at any cost – even their own sense of selves. Feminist posters line Molly and Amy's bedrooms, conversations about sexuality are confidently exclaimed, and there is near nothing standing in the girls' way, only the landscape of adulthood. It is an insistent open-mindedness that is, I suspect, a product of the longed-for liberalism that characterised much of the art that came out of Trump's America, offering a dreamland of unprompted acceptance that allows Wilde to make coming-of-age, and its pull on Molly and Amy's friendship, the singular dramatic tension. Miles away from Morrison and Ferrante, perhaps, *Booksmart* is nevertheless attuned in its own romanticised way to the mechanisms of adulthood that can complicate such intimacies. Almost all coming-of-age tales, after all, balance precariously on this precipice, peeping cautiously over its edge. In *Booksmart*, the possibilities that adulthood affords is contingent on Molly and Amy accepting the dislocation of both time and space that will occur as they depart on separate paths. Yet, there is a future in this new malleability, the film reminds us: the safety net of girlhood may be removed but its knots of intimacy can – and do – persist.

'We could never have loved the earth so well if we had had no childhood in it,' writes George Eliot in her 1860 novel *The Mill on the Floss*. 'What novelty is worth that sweet monotony, where everything is known and *loved* because it is known?'[12] I am reminded suddenly of these words, and they stir a buried network of friendship in my mind. I trace it back slowly, through the fictional sisterhoods it binds together: spoken to Beth by Saoirse Ronan's Jo in *Little Women*, who played Beanie Feldstein's best friend in *Lady Bird*, who went on to star in *Booksmart*.

Across the canon of coming-of-age stories, a line of young women stretches, their hands clasped, caught together in the violent throes of adolescent transformation. Through the unquiet commotion of their intimacies, they summon a new cultural climate, one that points to a richer and more radical imagination of female interiority than what came before. It has been centuries now since the Bildungsroman first suggested that it is not only who but how we become that is important, that the slow bloom of a character's psychological life could be the entire plot. I am, long past my own childhood, so grateful for the answering echo: that it is not only how but with whom that determines our lives. In the journey from childhood monotony to the novel wilderness of adulthood, it is sometimes our only guide; a cartography of our inaugural impulses towards intimacy, of our raw, emerging, enmeshed selves.

Chapter 2
Physical intimacy

When she was 21, my best friend died in a car accident that left debris behind on a remote Northern Ireland road and made the front page of our local newspaper for a week before it disappeared from the physical evidences of the world altogether. In the months that followed, I would reread old messages between us with a pallid, exhausted obsession: the casual exchanges from the days before it happened, the last message sent when she was already dead. She loved *Anne of Green Gables* but I read *Little Women* at her funeral because I liked it more, and thus thought it might articulate better the sudden absolute desolation that I felt. I still don't know, after all these years, if that was the wrong thing to do.

I spent so much time trying to understand what happened in words and thought – the books on grief piled up, the memories summoned and reimagined, the circumstances of her death reasoned over and over again in notebooks and on scraps of paper. But language, I learned, is a weak and indolent thing; inadequate for charting the interminable landscapes of grief, useless for holding the fading flicker of someone in your mind. 'You learn how much grief is about language,' Chimamanda Ngozi Adichie writes about the death of her father, 'the failure of language and the grasping for language.'[1] Language failed me again and again. Conversations between us collapsed into the vague pulp of childhood until I could barely remember her voice, and I was no longer sure of the person she was or might have become. I struggled to make anyone understand the sudden dismembering of it all. I struggled to make even myself understand.

Somehow all that was left – all that felt certain – was the sheer, irrevocable *thereness* of her before: the muscle memory of her once-aliveness, a testament to our collective existence in a palpable, undeniable world. Her ghost took on the muteness and fragmentation of a photograph album, a series of abrupt synecdoches that came to signal the ragged endurance of her in my mind: the wide cut of her smile, a burgundy T-shirt pulled against the flat of her stomach, her hands – cheerfully broad nail beds and delicately wrought knuckles. They say you know something as well as the back of your hand but I think it is still the back of hers that I would know best, that I would recognise even after so many years of grief and misremembering and forgetting.

It took her absence from the slow turn of this world for me to realise that friendship is, and has always been, a physical proposition, a corporeal act that occurs between people – their bodies and desires and tangible, quotidian realities. I think I understood, perhaps, in a small way before; the urgency of proximity, the unspoken promise of accessibility that undergirds almost every act of intimacy. In Ann Brasheres' young adult book series *The Sisterhood of the Travelling Pants*, one of the eponymous sisterhood writes of her friends: 'We forget where one of us starts and the other one stops. When Tibby sits next to me in the movies, she bangs her heel against my shin… Usually I don't even notice until the bruise blooms the next day.'[2] Their friendships are inscribed across limbs, writ large against blood vessels and layers of skin. It set the standard for how I imagined friendship to be, but I still didn't realise what a primary, necessary component it was until it was gone.

The idea of physical intimacy amongst friends is not taboo, precisely, but it is perhaps the least understood form of platonic affection, because such intimacy still doggedly belongs to the realm of romantic and sexual relationships. During the COVID-19 pandemic – especially in the jolt of the first lockdown, when the wounds of our upheaval were still fresh enough to bear investigation – I would scroll through the internet, past dozens of articles shared across tabloids and art magazines and lifestyle websites alike, all asking the same thing: what would happen to the world of sex, dating, and relationships in this brave new world? How would single people cope with this paradigm of touch-starvation that had overnight become public health policy? There was, of course, very little consideration for how people who depended on physical comfort from their friends would manage. That kind of touch, the kind that wasn't erotic, or romantic, or heteronormative, had already long been deemed disposable.

But friendships are, of course, distinctly physical, carnal things. Carnal – from the Latin *carnalis*, meaning of the flesh. They remind us of our embodied existence in this world, of the essentially mortal, human, meaty business of binding your life to another person, whether platonically or romantically. In Emma Jane Unsworth's 2014 novel *Animals*, best friends Laura and Tyler populate each other's bodies through a drug-addled friendship that constructs a brand-new ecosystem of shared corporeality: the same substances smeared across nostrils, the same fluids shared, the same dank, matted bedclothes rolled into. Reading the book is itself a bodily undertaking; the evocation of cocaine and MDMA at the back of the nasal cavity, the dry glue of a hangover in the mouth, the reality of another body's choices seeping through your own. True to the book's title, the epon-ymous Laura and Tyler are feral, untamed creatures, sniffing at themselves and leaving a trail of waste in their wake, their primal instincts animating their friendship and their lives.

Their symbiotic experience of the world – 'I wondered whether we'd been fucking simultaneously in beds across town, our lives in split-screen,'[3] Laura writes after a text from Tyler one morning – is thrown into disarray when Laura meets pianist Jim and, in quick succession, falls in love and becomes engaged. While she desperately tries to maintain her ties to Tyler, their shared experience of the debauched pleasures of the body – pleasure shared, pleasure doubled – begins to fragment. In the 2019 film adaptation directed by Sophie Hyde, it is at first impossible to tell next to whose dark, curly head Laura is lying; a queer kind of slippage that is slowly replaced by the omnipresence of her in Jim's bed. Acquaintances begin insistently to ask the women about pregnancy and children, reminding them of the incompatibility of their lifestyles with motherhood. Jim disapproves of Laura's antics with Tyler, of the dispersal of her body between them. 'I don't understand why it has to be just him,' Tyler comments bitterly in the film, feeling Laura slipping away. 'He's not enough.' The transition that became apparent in the previous chapter – the expected graduation from friendship to monogamous partnership

– is a transition that is also cast in the body, in who can inhabit the real estate of a woman's physical practices.

If female intimacy has always been determined by the patriarchy's desires, then the female and feminised body are the battleground through which this control has been wrested. The narratives constructed around these bodies – as sexual objects and maternal vessels and almost nothing in between – map directly onto the structuring principles of the patriarchy: the economic and social disempowerment of marginalised genders, the proliferation of the nuclear family, and the provision of free domestic labour. Acts of physical intimacy and pleasure that don't directly reinforce these structures, that suggest the possibility of self-determination, pose an immediate threat; we saw the panicked response to such progress in the recent global stripping back of reproductive and queer rights. This was a blunt reminder to us all: the patriarchal state can, at any point, commandeer your body to dispossess you of political agency. You cannot act on the hedonism of your desires. You cannot divorce the intricacy of your gender from the supposed directive of your sex. You cannot move through society with the full knowledge of a physical and psychic reality that is yours to grasp. 'It is not so much the notion of our own inferiority that we women have internalized,' writes Virginie Despentes in her 2006 feminist manifesto *King Kong Theory*. 'It is the idea that our independence is destructive that has penetrated to the marrow of our bones.'[4]

We are taught our independence is destructive, and so we are taught to be pliable – to fit neatly into relationships and against men, to hold children to our chests and lose all claim to our bodies whatsoever. Yet the reclamation of our interiorities lies within this very body, in the autonomy that thrives when placing it in new contexts of vulnerability, wanting, and care. The long history of abortion cinema, and its emphasis on moments of physical interdependence in the face of an unyielding state, aligns the reclamation of the body's intimacies with the reclamation of its reproductive agency, and thus demonstrates the radical effect of such alternative attachments on both the political body and the body politic. There, we have Baby holding Penny tight before her termination in 1987's *Dirty Dancing*, Autumn reaching out to touch Skylar's hand in Eliza Hittman's 2020 independent film *Never Rarely Sometimes Always*, Amina putting herself in harm's way to obtain her daughter an illegal procedure in Mahamet-Saleh Haroun's 2021 Chadian drama *Lingui*. This mutually implicated experience of the body, and the resilience and comfort of touch, can become a site of resistance and restoration. It can shift the boundaries between where one person begins and another ends, where empathy becomes solidarity becomes experience.

The isolation of the pandemic made all this tender and precise in my mind, like the sharp, bloody topography of a fresh scratch, legible against the fingertips. I felt the gap between my friends and myself acutely, our intimacies reduced to typed out messages and muffled encounters outside, standing far apart on the frozen grass and stone of our emptied cityscape. It was around this time, with so many days and weeks on my hands and none of them valuable, that I turned to *Girls*. Lena Dunham's television series about a group of twenty-something female friends is a clear response to an existing genre, from the zingy co-dependence of *Friends* to the sleek modernity of *Sex and the City*, about young people navigating sex, careers, and families against the flurry of New York City. But in *Girls*, the relationships between its characters are messier, at times spiteful to behold. No canned laughter soundtracks the world of Lena Dunham's Hannah, Alison Williams' Marnie, Jemima Kirke's Jessa, and Zosia Mamet's Shoshanna, no cosy cafés and recurring in-jokes construct an easy camaraderie around their lives. In the vein of Ferrante's Lenù and Lila, very little kindness is exchanged between them – it is difficult to think of a more careless group of people since F. Scott Fitzgerald put pen to paper. At a time when life felt so apathetic, when friendships had been condensed to enforced distance and unending aimlessness, *Girls* made a sick kind of sense.

On the surface, the characters' various encounters with men propel the show, and much has been made over the years about *Girls'* landmark, near grotty depiction of sex, in which bodies look unwieldy and the most provocative of fantasies become nothing more than a negotiated encounter between bits of flesh. Yet, during the lonely disquiet of the world ending, I was struck by how this unceremonious intimacy translates across all of the show's relationships, so that the friendships between the characters are born not out of affection or even choice, but through such naturalised tactility that intimacy becomes an inevitability. *Girls* reclaimed the body; it reclaimed it from the voyeuristic imagination of the male gaze; it even reclaimed it, as Jia Tolentino argued in the New Yorker[5] from an audience intent on judging the suitability of the characters as partners, parents, or indeed people. Most of all, it wrenched back the physicality of friendship, slipping it into a guise that felt barely recognisable. There are few air kisses and hugs between the girls (the *women*) of *Girls*, few sentimental, curled-up moments on beat-up sofas. Instead, they dance in the same room when they can barely stomach to speak to each other. They gingerly hold hands or resentfully sit next to another in distress. They – in one scene I think of often – sit in the same bathtub as one silently sobs after a failed marriage and splashes snot into the bath water – submerged in fluids, the gaps between selves dissolving.

Hannah, Marnie, Jessa & Shoshanna. I imagine their names stacked on one of those T-shirts, a portrait of a group simultaneously adjacent and detached. They don't have the kind of friendship to which anyone would particularly aspire; I am frustrated constantly by the facile, childish ways they squabble for illusory scraps of political power. And yet, I cannot shake the rude wilfulness of their bodies from my mind, the ways that their insufficient, narcissistic intimacies understand the body, and the concomitant friendship it enacts, not as an endless source of feminine alliance, but as a means for expression when language fails. Here we are, again, at wordlessness. In *Girls*, language fails the characters; or perhaps, more accurately, they fail language, unable to dredge up the words to attend to each other's distinct, emotionally complex personhoods. But even in the extremes of their self-absorption, their bodies articulate an impulse toward collectivity – a flash of looking and embodying beyond the self.

'I don't know what you're feeling. I won't even pretend.'[6] I think of this line, in relation to the broken, ineloquent friendships in *Girls*; I think of it in relation to us all. I think of what can be experienced through the body – the delirious heat of its desires, the tacky mire of its frustrations, the intransigence of its changes as we age – and how impossible these sensations are to communicate, to reach across the divide of language and try and express: 'This has happened, and this, and this.' I stretch my body against my friend's on the sofa and fit my chin against her hipbone. I walk down the street, twist my wrist and clench the knuckles of my hand tight against my palm. I lean my forehead against my friend's knee, slumped against the floor. 'I don't know what you're feeling.' It rings in my head. 'I won't even pretend.'

The line comes from Jeffrey Eugenides' 1993 novel *The Virgin Suicides*, a fairy tale of haunted American suburbia that follows five sisters – Cecilia, Lux, Bonnie, Mary, and Therese Lisbon – who, one by one, kill themselves under the close suffocation of their adolescence. A novel about sisters that nevertheless defies everything the nuclear family stands for, *The Virgin Suicides* is, in many ways, a study into the failures of empathy, a documentation of the refusal of anyone – the girls' parents who increasingly place them under stricter isolation; the group of avid, pubescent boys who pine for and narrate the sisters from afar – to try and understand their unhappiness. This particular line occurs in a condolence card addressed to the parents after the suicide of their youngest daughter Cecilia, but I remember it so often because I have, over the years, misremembered it, thought it said perhaps by one of the boyish narrators in an attempt to get close to the girls, or by Cecilia's doctor in penitence for his infamously condescending words after her initial suicide attempt ('What are you doing here, honey? You're not even old enough to know how bad life gets'[7]). I think, in a way, that I was right, that it maybe is; a sly, deliberate misattribution of grief from Eugenides, a displacement of concern and understanding. What would have happened if someone had addressed these words to the lonely sisters, shut up like rotting flowers inside their rooms? What might have been prevented?

As it is, however, no one does. Throughout the novel, the narrators – the boys of the girls' youth and the forlorn, fixated adults they become – excavate their fantasy of the sisters' interiorities, searching for an existential answer to explain the sudden violence the girls unleash upon themselves, the determination with which they, quietly and unobtrusively, call an end to their fledgling lives. 'In the end we had the pieces of the puzzle,' they say, 'but no matter how we put them together, gaps remained, oddly shaped emptinesses mapped by what surrounded them, like countries we couldn't name.'[8] And yet, these boy-men never edge close to the truth; that perhaps the answer does not lie in the pilfered diaries and confidential medical records amassed, nor in the second- and third-hand testimonials collected from old male classmates, related with the arrogance of certitude. That perhaps the answer lies in five controlled bodies, impossible to live within and yet possible to escape. These are the lacunae that the narrators cannot bridge or even fully chart: the suppression of the Lisbon sisters' soft, thrumming sexuality, the ordained shame of a developing body covered in a shapeless dress, the gradual, impassive way the girls eventually collapse into themselves – and each other.

In the 1999 film adaptation by Sofia Coppola, the increasingly tangible conditions of the Lisbon sisters' isolation are palpable, translated by a filmmaker who has always understood the political power of the material. Coppola's film-making is unnerving in its sensuality, a staleness filling the screen and throat as the camera pans over the girls shut together, the very light through the windows dusty and muted. Their room and the stairs up to it are slippery and spiky with clutter – sheer stockings draped over bannisters, discarded picture cards and perfume bottles littering surfaces – their environment simultaneously expressive and oppressive. Somewhere, an old, half-eaten sandwich sits on the floor. The girls are almost always in pyjama shorts or nightgowns, no matter the time of day, a tired mustiness filling the air.

No one addresses words of comfort to the girls and so they, in their own way, say them to each other, through the closed gap of legs and hips and waists. The easy familiarity seen in the rare moments that the girls collide with the outside world – brushing each other's hair before a school dance, giggling as they tease a boy – intensifies into a far more bodily attachment in their mandated isolation, lying piled together, bare wrists and thighs entangled, stroking each other's hair. Similar to the friendship group in *Girls*, the Lisbon sisters eschew emotional communication for physical co-existence – the boys note that even when the remaining sisters file past Cecilia's open coffin, their faces are 'dazed and expressionless.'[9] And eventually, this single, osmotic mass of sisterhood is not enough. Together, the girls feel the relentless pull of the exhaust smoke and the sleeping pills that literalise a fixed end to what Ann Backman Rogers argues are the 'small doses of death that are dealt to young girls' throughout our lives.[10] Eventually, they decide to end it all, the damp skin and insistent breath of their bodies together. It is, perhaps, the only recourse to control they feel they have left.

Over the years, accusations of glamourising suicide have been levelled at Coppola and, to a lesser extent, Eugenides (perhaps because he is a man, perhaps because he does not trade in the often easily mistakable superficiality of aesthetic that Coppola does). But *The Virgin Suicides*, despite the sharp shock of its name, is less about the moment of death than about the position of the female body in life, about the ways it is a pregnable barrier to both unwelcome intrusion and collective experience. Throughout the novel, the sisters' bodies are dragged into the public sphere against their will – belonging to the boys, belonging to their parents – a blank canvas against which the town's anxieties and curiosities and burning, shameful longings can be projected and rearranged and understood. But they also belong to themselves and to each other. The grotesquery of their sisterly pact is not so much a victory of control, but a demonstration of the inevitable end point when the collective female body is contorted according to another's needs. Legible here is the intimacy of trauma, of isolation, of what happens when only a handful of people can, without pretending, understand how you might feel. The same loneliness runs through the Lisbon sisters' veins, the same clog of the shuttered household in their chests. When the film's Lux, in a rare moment of articulation, tries to appeal to her mother in the days before their end, her voice is disembodied from her girlish form. 'We're suffocating,' she says, desperate and choked. 'I can't breathe in here.' She is speaking for them all – the intimacy of knowing the fragility of another's form.

There are times when, like the Lisbon sisters, my body feels like an imposition, like an inherited property over which I have no say, in which I am merely kept, and monitored, and maintained. I am tired of thinking about it, about its possibilities and its failures, tired of tracking the futility of sickening desires and anxieties that I cannot quiet or contain, tired of the way that my agency seems to dissolve against the barriers of my skin – that the things I want and believe rarely seem to translate. But there are also times when, like in *Animals*, I am almost winded by the invisible static that seems to exist between my friends' bodies and my own, by the sudden energy pounding in my blood, by the dizzying liberation suddenly promised.

I stumble out into the night during the August festivals; I stretch out my arms and feel the warm, heavy air against my fingertips. I press the flat of my hand against the top of my friend's head; they reach back and pull my arm around. For years now, the main refuge that I have found from the strangled panic in my mind has been here. I can take my body and tuck it away – hidden and hushed – from the dictates of all the narratives that make it feel inept and undone. Friendship has always been a physical proposition – I learnt this long ago – an encounter between breathing, heart-pounding bodies. It is not possible to separate it from the politics of the body that dominate the rest of our lives. Amid the amphitheatre of female spectacle that constitutes our reality, there is a defiance to this language of silence, of reclaimed and wilfully rearticulated desire. It takes up the long-decided script of our skin and blood and flesh; it strikes out what came before and writes anew.

Chapter 3
Personhood

When I am in need of comfort, or ease, or sheer brains-off tranquillity, I turn to the television shows of my childhood and adolescence. This – the post-Cold War era marked by a flush, neoliberal optimism, the post-9/11 era marked by an urge toward predictability and pleasure – was the heyday of the sitcom and procedural, where everything would unfold precisely as it was meant to: the same familiar faces, the same regular timeslots, the same storylines skating neatly along like a tram following its tracks. Week in, week out, House would diagnose a hopeless case five minutes before the episode ended, the friends from *Friends* would congregate at Central Perk, and the ragtag team in *Castle* would investigate a new, sanitised murder. Everyone hung out in the same bars and workplaces, everyone dated each other, and no real world existed beyond the boundaries of the cast and the occasional guest appearance. It was a retreat from reality, a flirtation with alternative forms of relation, that became, in many ways, nothing more than a reproduction of the typical family unit in microcosm: a gentle, innocuous co-dependency that sustained our idea of community as a series of strict, constraining structures.

Yet amidst all this, Cristina Yang turned to her best friend Meredith Grey in *Grey's Anatomy* and explained that, when filling out the paperwork for her abortion, she had written Meredith's name on the form as her emergency contact. 'That's why I told you I'm pregnant,' Cristina tells her. 'You're my person.' I don't know if anyone could have predicted the effect this line, spoken unsentimental and frank, would have; the way it would refrain and echo between the women through the long years of the show and bleed into our popular lexicon – inscribed on mugs and keyrings, tenderly promised in wedding vows. And although I don't particularly like *Grey's Anatomy* (a show populated by some of the most insufferable people in television history) and although the show was as guilty as any other of its time in reaffirming the conventional claustrophobia of the nuclear community, I remain fascinated by this phrase, by what it says about how we conceptualise friendship structures and the nature of intimacy within female selfhood.

What does it mean to be someone's person? There is a practicality to it, as there was for Cristina and Meredith; a sense that this is a primary safety net, a designated safe space in the world. But it also has a wilder, more expansive implication; a categorisation that slips past the social into something almost ontological. To be someone's person suggests a tribal entanglement, a tender and elective citizenship within another's intimacies – a nationhood of friendship. It is both an affective declaration – a retelling of the word soulmate liberated from its romantic trappings – and a profoundly political affirmation: an acknowledgement of shared humanity. It releases intimacy from the confines of the nuclear family unit by asserting that such intimacy exists and occurs naturally within our very personhood, eschewing the artificial structures that seek to claim it. Person, of course, is the singular form of people, a word that is itself both singular and plural. To be someone's person is to become a common people, a collective assemblage of individual lives.

In her female friendship memoir *Text Me When You Get Home*, cultural critic Kayleen Schaefer argues that depictions of alternative families in television were popularised during the 1990s by a generation who 'no longer looked to work for fulfilment or respected authority figures the way their parents had.'[1] This rupture had, I think, trickled down from the more radical politics of the Gay Liberation movement and particularly the AIDS crisis in the US, both of which had reformulated conservative conceptualisations of community into queered patchworks of found family. The flitty urban families of the likes of *Friends* and *Seinfeld* and *ER* to an extent appropriated this shift; they condensed its burlesque, heterogenous possibilities back into the rigidity of the nuclear family. The friendship of personhood reappropriates right back. It imagines what might happen if, as seminal queer theorist Eve Kosofsky Sedgwick asks, 'the richest junctures weren't the ones where everything *means the same thing*?'[2] What might happen if we construct communities that undo the fixity of the family unit, that uncover intimacy within our most primal urgencies. What might happen if we think of our very personhood as a relational and deeply attached thing.

I have often, particularly in the chaos of my late twenties and early thirties, been struck by the almost impossibility of my person; a disorientation that manifests frequently as a sensation of collapse. I notice it especially when I am unhappy, as if my mind were draining away, and in the acuteness of longing, as if the edges of myself were magmatic, melting into air. *I want him so much I think my skin is dissolving*, I write to a friend. *I'm so tired I can feel my brain leaking into my skull* (I am very dramatic). What I am saying, I suppose, is that I am not always sure of the solidity of myself as a person, particularly in moments of extreme emotion; a natural condition of being human, perhaps, where the immensity of one's interiority hardly seems containable, quantifiable, or reasonable in any way. To be not only your own person but also someone else's under such conditions seems both a wild and irrational proposition and a natural and obvious inevitability. It is a fundamentally unstructured act, beyond anything that any administrative social unit could signify. Or perhaps it is structured, but with the daring of an Escher painting; spaces attached not through logic or order but through the undeniable veracity of a connection, a staircase drawing two points tight together across impossible planes.

In Issa Rae's television show *Insecure*, this kind of sticky sweet clan-making unfolds both within and across lines of identity, pulling and unpulling settled forms of relation and creating new and needed communities. The show follows the close friendship between old college friends Issa, played by Rae herself, and Yvonne Orji's Molly, and their wider college group, as they navigate the ongoing chaos of late-twenties-early-thirties (re)coming-of-age in a humming Los Angeles. A milestone in Black storytelling in television, *Insecure* strove to communicate a portrait of the Black experience that did not derive dramatic tension through oppression but, as Rae explained, 'regular Black people living life.'[3] Such familiarity and loose, generous belonging are pressed deep into the seams of the show, locating intimacy in the mutual recognition of personhood and a shared tread through the world.

Both Issa and Molly, and their wider network, live in an undeniably white world, thrown into sharp relief by both the oblivious, often ludicrous gaucheness of their workplaces (Molly, a high-powered law firm; Issa initially a non-profit aimed at disenfranchised Black youth entirely headed by white people) and the broader culture around them (in almost every season, the characters binge television parodying the oftentimes clumsy racial politics of real-life shows such as *Scandal* or true crime dramas). The moments between the women become an exhale from the sometimes disorienting, sometimes laughable nonsense of these spaces. Their friendships articulate themselves through their own language; Issa and Molly, in the tradition of the most starry-eyed of couples, finish each other's sentences, speak quickly in codewords, wordlessly turn up on the other's doorstep with supplies and apologies and comfort. When, in the first episode, Issa performs 'Broken Pussy', a rap she wrote based on Molly's romantic disasters, even this breach of trust is made possible through the tight tangle of their bond. To be someone's person is to hold a particular kind of knowledge and a particular kind of power – a Rosetta Stone of another's silent insecurities and wants. If intimacy is a practised familiarity, *Insecure* is a study in how another's personhood is familiarised, how it can be learned by heart.

Yet for all the secret language of their intimacy, the relationships in *Insecure* are an ode to friendship that is outward-looking and encompassing, rather than navel-gazing and insular; considering how the careful connection held between separate people could make even the most neglected interiorities bright and legible. It expands rather than contracts worlds: the relationships form a vibrant, prickly, worn-in portrait of Black sisterhood that pulls others in; by the end of the show, Issa has left the reliably microaggresive non-profit to set up a bloc party that supports and platforms Black artists. Certainly, *Insecure* is a show about friendship, but it is also markedly about community, and the radical world-making of a connection when a person is entirely seen and understood by another. There is an inherent generosity of spirit here that feels – even in this golden age of television – rare, that I can only mark in a handful of other places. Crystal Moselle's *Betty*, in which a band of skater girls determine to organise an all-girls meet-up, and whose first season ends not with the core gang but with dozens of girls and femmes flying through the streets of New York on their skateboards, arms stretched towards the sky and each other; or Laure Nunn's *Sex Education*, in which a group of schoolgirls, many of whom can barely stand each other, congregate together on a bus after one of them is sexually assaulted on her journey to school.

What we are edging towards is an imagination of female friendship rooted in solidarity rather than family: friendship that determines to uphold and have stake in another's personhood, to uncover the ways in which vulnerabilities and experiences and desires are aligned both within and across pre-existing bonds. Solidarity, of course, is a largely political – and specifically leftist – idea, used to describe a state of perpetual willingness to act that braces the relationship between political comrades, by collectivising subjugation and the response towards it. It ought, I think, to be used carefully in relation to friendship; they are not interchangeable ideas and treating them as such can erase both the independently political possibility of friendship and the essentially disaffected nature of comradeship – one need not be friends with, or even like, a person to be in political solidarity with them. But there is nevertheless a marked and beguiling slippage between the two that points to the inherently radical possibilities of both – their latent insubordination, the liberation they locate within human connection.

There is admittedly not a great deal of space for such radical thinking in the largely mainstream landscape of television; although I cannot help thinking again of Moselle's *Betty*, which is so unapologetically queer, unapologetically plural – where kids tack up Black Lives Matter posters and squat in abandoned gentrified buildings to create community centres, whose entire narrative thrust centres on bringing people in rather than shutting them out. It is a show not so much responding to a political context as it is defined by it; finding both endearing, natural affection and ground-breaking camaraderie in the friendships between the girls, *Betty* stages a quiet revolution – feminist, queer, working class – by reclaiming the streets of New York through community-building. 'Skateboarding has always been on the fringe: it was for the misfits and people on the outskirts who don't want to be part of mainstream society,' Moselle has said. 'Now it's inclusive of people who feel a certain way inside that they felt before they couldn't express.'[4] Far beyond the prim parochiality of the urban family drama, *Betty* refashions the hang-out show into something lawless: friendship as community, care as action, intimacy decentralised and spinning joyously through the streets.

There is a fundamental optimism to this kind of friendship, that discovers intimacy within the very essence of personhood and engages to attend to it for no other reason than the instinct and volition of the self. Such radical intimacy makes viable an inherently emancipatory politics, opening up new possibilities not just of connection, but of security, dignity, and empowerment. Ridley Scott's seminal 1991 film *Thelma and Louise* is ostensibly a road trip drama about two eponymous friends on the run after one kills for the other, but is really a wry consideration of how such ride-or-die attachment can implement restorative justice after a lifetime of male violence. In 1980's satire *9 to 5*, three women (real-life friends Jane Fonda, Lily Tomlin, and Dolly Parton), initially taught to be suspicious of each other, band together to wreak revenge on their lecherous boss. *Daughters of the Dust*, the first feature film directed by an African-American woman to get theatrical distribution in the United States, visualises with dreamlike sensibility the kind of negotiations and care a community of Gullah islanders – mothers, sisters, lovers and friends – must undertake as they prepare to leave their island for the first time post-slavery. Explicitly political, meanwhile, is Yara Rodrigues Fowler's 2022 novel *there are more things*, centring two women – Brazilian PhD student Catarina and second-generation Brazilian-Londoner Melissa – whose slow-blooming friendship is scaffolded by their activism in the wake of Brexit, austerity, and the impeachment of Brazilian President Dilma Rousseff. The entanglement of their solidarity – both personal and political – transforms the expected portrait of millennial urban friendship into an investigation of the paths of intimacy that trace the long road towards progressive change. There is a quiet revolution, literal and unliteral, that such intimacies make possible – that rescue female political agency and selfhood from their battered past.

As I write this, there is a revolution of a sort happening – although I think there maybe always is, somewhere in the world. But this one is taking place where I am from, which feels different, although perhaps it shouldn't. In Iran, protests and clashes, led by women and girls, have been erupting for months in response to the murder of a young woman, Jina Mahsa Amini, by the regime's morality police. And in the awful safety of the internet, I have been watching them unfold, so dazed with the fear of what might come to pass that I hardly feel real. Where to even begin with the weight of it. I find I don't know how; because it is in progress, and so far away, and all I really have is the news, which is brusque and unfeeling, and social media, which is incomplete, and I am simply not there, which feels like a failure of character in a way it never had before. Mostly I am angry, and heartsick, and overwhelmed by the immensity of our inherited loss: entire futures snatched away, the exiled past inaccessible, the present an ongoing impossibility. I was born in the twelfth year of the Islamic Republic, and now, in a handful of years, before the turn of the new decade, it will turn fifty. This, too, does not seem real.

It has always been strange to have the edges of yourself demarcated by negative space, by where you are not and can never go. For years now, the diasporic nature of my identity – born in the UK, never set foot in Iran, always in between and nowhere – feels like a barrier that has rendered parts of myself obscure; a pane of dense, frosted glass through which home is perceptible, but shadowy and distorted and slyly out of reach. Watching the news, I feel wretched with helplessness and also deeply aware of my own lack of repercussion, my entire safe removal from almost any consequence of what is unfolding – the doubled protection and cost of unbelonging. The protests go on, and I go about my own days, and in the midst of this, I find myself drawn back, after many years, to Azar Nafisi's memoir *Reading Lolita in Tehran*, a book which feels suddenly, desperately present. I page through it in abrupt, brief flashes on the rattle of the Tube during a trip to London; it is in my bag as I pass by a protest in Trafalgar Square, the amber gold of a lion rippling on a flag and the familiar chants in my mouth. Much like in the book, the boundaries between literature and the world seep like liquid and I feel entirely disoriented, as if I am both there and not there: in Tehran, in Iran, where the ground is shaking with collective female rage and where maybe, after so long, something might change.

Reading Lolita in Tehran is a 'memoir in books', written by literature professor Nafisi and tracing her life in the immediate aftermath of the 1979 revolution to her eventual relocation to the United States in the 1990s. The title is named for a secret book club that Nafisi starts with a group of mostly female students (one of the student's husbands also cheerfully attends from time to time) after she leaves teaching at the university, in which they read banned works of Western literature. The act of reading *Lolita* in Tehran – of discovering Vladimir Nabokov's cunning critiques of power, of engaging with art as determined mutiny – forms the thrust of Nafisi's recollections. But reading it this time, I find myself fascinated not so much by the literary discussions as the intimacy they carve out, the quiet revolution taking place in another's living room.

Gathering in Nafisi's flat, the women slowly disrobe themselves, thick black chadors and scarves unwrapped and glimpses of colour marking each of the students out. They are, initially, deeply fragmented – a group of loners who for years found safety in solitude, the women are clumsy with each other and themselves, sharply divided across politics and beliefs and unused to the vulnerability and boldness that such intimacy, by necessity, demands. As they spend more time with each other and delve into the tender exposure of each other's responses to art and life, as they build small, gentle routines of tea and pastries and existing freely within the same space, they come to build a dependency that resists the force of the state as much as their clandestine dealings with forbidden literature. The women increasingly spend time in Nafisi's home, welcomed by her family and becoming a regular fixture. They innately understand the gendered violence of state law: when one of their number Sanaz is punished, or Nafisi's small daughter has a traumatic encounter, the group flock around en masse, with words of comfort and stories of their own. '*Madame Bovary* had done what years of teaching at the university had not,' Nafisi says, looking around at her students sharing dinner with her family. 'It created a shared intimacy.'[5]

Fascism and totalitarianism have always been concerned with a colonisation of the imagination, shrinking down the perimeters of what we see as possible. 'We had become the figment of someone else's dreams,' Nafisi explains of the new Islamic Regime. 'He had come in the name of a past, a past that, he claimed, had been stolen from him. And he now wanted to re-create us in the image of that illusory past.'[6] Yet *Reading Lolita in Tehran* speaks back at the decades-long capture of this shared imagination, pulling at its bunched up, constricted form and seizing it as a tool for radical collectivity and, through this, liberation. In one chapter, Nafisi speaks directly to the reader, intent on taking them past the room of the book group and into the public spaces of the city through one of her student's imagined journeys home. In doing so, Nafisi pulls us into another woman's interiority, crafting a shared psychic space that demands we consider not only what this woman experiences, as she walks quickly and quietly through the streets alone, but what she is feeling: fear at the hostility of the streets, humiliation and loss at a country that has been pulled from her grasp. It is a moment of solidarity, but also of a collapse of boundaries – between the women who walk the pathways of the book and those who follow their written steps. It is in this readiness to dream and act for each other that a reclamation of power lies. Such communal space – real and imagined – can, as Nafisi says, create its own intimacy. An openness to mutual implication that points to our willingness to be there for others, to stand ground, to merge.

There is a concept that I discovered recently, that I have been thinking about a lot. It is the desire path: the unplanned, unforeseen trails that spring up in parks and wildernesses and that are created by erosion and repeated footfall, by the determination of people to carve out their own way. These are the dusty routes that I walk on when I am crossing the city through the Meadows, that slant beneath my feet, that offer a new way forward; one that is more in the middle of things, through grass and around awkward stone and tree. I love these paths, and I love that we named them, and I love that we chose this name. Desire paths: the paths that we want, the ones that come into being not out of any clever, organising idea, but out of the instinctive movement of the people, the ways that they want to go.

When I think of the women in *Reading Lolita in Tehran*, of the strange, eager declaration of 'you're my person', of the intimacies that have been formed through sympathy and the elective tangle of distinct selfhoods, I am reminded all over again of these desire paths, of the routes towards community and emancipation that women have stamped out beyond the determined structures that seek to organise their lives. Thrust as we are along the familiar, narrow alleyways of relation that have long delineated our intimacies, our friendships can sprout gnarled, secret paths over and into which we can scramble – a wilful defiance of the ordained way of things. These paths reorient the geographies of our lives, and lay a new, longed for road beneath our feet. A shift, and a step, and suddenly everything becomes possible: solidarity, revolution, the strange immensity of our personhoods, so hard for even ourselves to understand. A dissolution of the self, both contained and uncontained, spilling out over the grass, going somewhere new.

Chapter 4
The breakup

Almost every autumn, it seems, I find myself back in my old university city, engaged in a wary kind of negotiation with my own nostalgia. The season seems to have a different quality here; the light limpid and golden-bright, the air sharp and somehow burnt – the kind of cold snap that catches in the throat. I love it here desperately, but in a searching, spectral way, like a tourist passing through a place that no longer exists; relict standing stones from a disappeared past. If I try very hard, I can almost pretend as if the years haven't passed, and the altered shop fronts and blocks of brand-new city haven't dissolved and reassembled before my eyes. Everything here reminds me of beginnings – the bewitching high of early adulthood when anything felt possible, when every person felt like a catalyst that might rewrite the intimacies of an entire life – which makes it an odd, and also fitting, place to now house so many endings. Strange, really, that the academic year starts when the rest of the year is dying away. Sitting here, halfway through the rhythm of a first term that is not mine, the past feels dimensional, unravelling, as if the very air is rung through with dishevelled leaves and the bright, hopeful rubber of a new pencil case. Everywhere I look seems written in palimpsest, and I cannot, however hard I try, come to pull the layers of my life apart.

I have always had a difficult relationship with the past, which is to say that I have always had a difficult relationship with endings. I have never liked them, not since childhood, when I would skip the finales of television shows and refuse to read the concluding parts to familiar books. The past, it has always seemed to me, is a landscape of endings, of things that didn't continue into the now – a curtailed and haunted pastoral. It signals the fact of human life, along with its defining intimacies, as inescapably fragile, as inhabiting a particular and inflexible tense. What we are contending with here is good old-fashioned mortality, but I am still, always, startled by how this mortality is practised before the final stroke, by all the significant and insignificant losses that make up a life.

Here, in the corridors of my almost-adulthood, it is impossible not to think of endings, of everything that ended here, or ended just past here – all the deeply important friendships that at the time felt so clear, so determined, so insoluble. It can be a hard and maddening thing, to structure your life around a kind of intimacy that seems designed to end. Friendships, more than any other relationship, seem to arrive with a designated expiry date, a life cycle that we spend most of our youth watching come to a close. Families, we understand, are implicitly bound for life, wedding vows are promised for eternity; but friendships contain no such assurance, tied to the crescent phases of a life rather than its full wane. I have been made to understand their frailty all my life: you will (of course) drift from childhood friends, you will (of course) drift from university friends, you will (of course) drift from friends collected at parties and work, and soon there will be no more fresh waves of friends and you, along with everyone else, will sit and wonder why it is so hard to make friends in adulthood, and whether this is it.

I call it drifting – everyone calls it drifting – but it is really an atomisation. Somewhere in adulthood, the ideals of marriage and the nuclear family (re)take over, and this shift in the gears of our intimacies has inevitable material aftershocks: people are drawn out towards the suburbs, because family-sized housing in the centre is expensive, they relocate to entirely new cities to prioritise partners and work, they have children and, in countries such as the UK with unaffordable childcare and no communal structures in place, are so often occupied with raising them alone. The underlying human momentum behind such changes can be wonderful – how nice to be in love and have a family and experience the vastness of the world – but over the centuries, patriarchal capitalism has stolen and warped the impulse of such affective behaviour, monopolising attention onto the mutually constituting practice of labour and the fragmented family unit.

Amidst the noise and chaos of our awful modernity, I find myself struck more and more by the non-neutrality of such attention, by the ways it forms its own world-making logic: the ways we pay attention to weddings, birth announcements, promotions; the ways we do not pay attention to the sudden madness of new desire, anniversaries of first meetings, the realisation of loose and feverish dreams. 'Patterns of attention – what we choose to notice and what we do not – are how we render reality for ourselves,' writes artist and writer Jenny Odell in *How To Do Nothing: Resisting the Attention Economy*, 'and thus have a direct bearing on what we feel is possible at any given time.'[1] Intimacy can only form its defining attachments through attention, through a co-presence of space and time; two fundamentals of human life that have been reified into commodity under capitalism and carefully bought up so as to keep women bound to the domestic sphere. So much of the life-altering, life-making ways in which I experienced intimacy in my adolescence and twenties is rendered unmanageable under these conditions: the spontaneous meet-ups and long nights spent talking and unceremonious involvement in another's everyday. It is near impossible to have a lack of ceremony, and all the ease it implies, without the wide, unregulated expanse of both space and time to render it natural. Everything becomes meticulously planned and then, eventually, not planned at all.

My friend sent me a TikTok some time ago, which – if I scroll through our messages – seems to constitute half our textual language. In it, a young person discusses alternative forms of spending time with friends that don't rely on spending money on coffees and lunches and trips away, that instead embed friendship in the quotidian rhythm of life. They use a framework that is new to me, radical in its tender mundanity: friends you might go on errands with. These are the friendships where quality time is constructed not through the luxurious artifice of time spent away from the responsibilities of life, but through the collective experience of these responsibilities, where doing the weekly grocery shop and filing taxes and working out are as much, and indeed more, an opportunity for intimacy as a mandated, bookended slot of leisure time.

I had never heard of the errand friend before, although I had unconsciously entrenched it within my life; my best friend's tread round the supermarket, the drape of her blue shopping bag, the brisk, methodical way she tessellates her groceries, are so familiar to me that sometimes I feel I am recalling them from the depths of childhood. But for a long time now, I have felt a resentment for the opposite of the errand friend: the kind of friendship that seems only to take place on occasions, that is lifted out of the everyday. I have, in my mind, dubbed this the brunch friendship; although this isn't particularly original or, indeed, fair – maybe it isn't kind to be petulant about others' joys. Yet, something about the idea of brunch – not the meal but the concept, the social structure, the exaggerated performance of middle-class femininity that it represents – sets me on edge. Perhaps it is its rigidity that feels emotionally impoverished, that undoes the queered, throwaway softness of the errand friend; the bulk of a table suddenly between two people, everything clothed in politeness and a synthetic glitz. It has come to signify everything I fear about how the friendships in my life might go: a bimonthly catch-up in a depersonalised space, the death rattle of what were once entangled lives, now pulled apart and frayed.

'Don't treat me like a three-hour brunch friend,' Frances Ha snaps at her best friend Sophie in Noah Baumbach's eponymously titled 2012 film *Frances Ha*, a late-coming-of-age story about two friends who fall apart. They are at a bar, after months of quintessential friendship drifting, and Frances has been getting steadily more drunk, and steadily more wounded at Sophie's distant, formal demeanour, at her boring interactions with her boring boyfriend Patch (how miserable to lose the love of your life to someone named Patch). Recognising their drifting and desperate to fix it, Frances clumsily bulldozes forward, trying to address the awkwardness head on and re-establish the old rules. But Sophie only looks weary. 'Really?' she asks. 'We're still doing this?' But Frances has never stopped doing this; never stopped believing in the magic of their friendship ('We're the same person with different hair,' she tells anyone who will listen), never stopped wanting things to remain exactly the same.

Co-written by Baumbach and the film's star Greta Gerwig, *Frances Ha* is a classic of mumblecore cinema, a subgenre of the American indie that finds drama and emotional propulsion in the everyday naturalism of people going about their lives. It is also widely considered one of the landmark friendship films, and in particular the friendship breakup film, treating the relationship between Frances and Sophie the way most would treat a romance, and giving weight to the trivial, unremarkable, and entirely heart-breaking mechanisms of their drifting. Frances is a sweet and hopeless person, aimless in the way one only can be in the liminality of twenties life, trying desperately to fix onto a performance of adulthood that seems always to elude her. She is so entirely useless at everything ('I'm just proud of myself for asking,' she tells her boss in an eager rush after her request for a promotion is gently rejected) that her friendship is the only thing that she seems to get right.

And how right it is. In a joyous opening montage, Frances and Sophie run full-pelt through the streets of New York, hands held and giddy, they read out loud to each other, they lean out of adjoining windows and smoke cigarettes, beaming across the short gap of plummeting air that separate them. Drenched in the soft black-and-white of the French New Wave, their lives are profoundly cinematic, and profoundly romantic; which is, perhaps, the problem. To Frances, her life with Sophie has the halcyon quality of a movie that no outside world can touch – 'tell me the story of us,' she asks childishly, tucked up in bed with Sophie, in love both with her friend and the fairy-tale they have made of their lives. She is entirely blindsided, then, when the unpleasant friction of reality intercedes, and when Sophie decided to move out. Here, in this abrupt shuffle, Baumbach and Gerwig lay bare the fear that perhaps lies at the heart of all intimacy: choosing someone who will not choose you back.

'Don't you think maybe they are the same thing,' Gerwig will go on to ask years later in her directorial debut *Lady Bird*, 'love and attention?' The seeds of her inquiry began early, in the ways that *Frances Ha* collates intimacy from all the fragments of a person that are so often invisible, and so often the central story. 'Then there are the details (which are the most important part, anyway),' Annie Baker writes in her Criterion essay on the film.[2] 'Sophie's glasses and the way they shine in the dark—how there's somehow always a little romantic light from Frances bouncing off of her. Frances's tendency to eat too fast.' In *Frances Ha*, what we pay attention to, and who we pay attention to, matter. Such details make up the tapestry of Frances' place in the world, and it is so difficult to watch it unspool so easily, as if it were an inevitability, or no big deal, or mere pragmatism. Frances tries, with very little success, to recreate her intimacy with Sophie: she stages a play-fight with an acquaintance, who is genuinely offended; she attends a fancy dinner party in which her whole self is overwritten by the efficient family lives of those around her. Everyone always seems to be telling her off – a park warden, a fellow university RA in her summer job. Overhanging her earnest, calamitous attempts at adulthood is a fear of doing life badly, and of doing life alone, which are, maybe, also the same thing.

Sophie moves out, and Frances has to learn – in her own words – how to become a real person, how to navigate the kind of heartbreak that no one seems to care about. Frances-and-Sophie becomes Frances Halliday, who eventually becomes Frances Ha – all that is visible on the nameplate of her new apartment – a newly born, half-interrupted person, forming both her own self and leaving space open for someone else. Frances finds work, choreographs her own dance show, and at the opening party catches a returned Sophie's eye – the kind of romantic lightning strike she had wistfully described to the dinner party's nonplussed audience. Frances and Sophie's intimacy morphs and adapts; and I know this is a good thing, but a part of me, the one that still runs away from the final telling of a story, misses the oversized T-shirts and bare legs of their communal living, the cigarettes and poetry and basking in the other's glow.

Perhaps what unsettles me most about *Frances Ha* is the sense that we should be passed what it shows, that this old story – the relinquishing of childish ways for an accomplished life – belongs to a different, unenlightened time. *Didn't we already do this?* I think, as everyone fragments into tidy units around me. *Didn't we devote decades to fighting this? Didn't we decide that this isn't what we want?* I spent my childhood reading the classic novels of English literature, arrogant with the birth right of my modernity. Jane Austen, the Brontës, Elizabeth Gaskell… their narratives were flush with a passion I yearned for, but the demands of their marriage plots, I felt with relief, would not, could never, concern me. I was so naïve, and so unprepared for the ways in which these things still deeply matter, the ways they still structure both our society and what we consider important. I had foolishly assumed that feminism, whatever abstracted understanding I had of it, had undone all this, that it had wiped the slate clean. That love could come without conditions; that we could dictate the open terms of our intimacies. I have spent years now in a state of irreconcilable desire, caught between stability and independence, subsumption and equity, entanglement and freedom.

In Claudia Weill's 1978 film *Girlfriends*, a direct predecessor to Baumbach's *Frances Ha*, such tension forms part of the self-determining struggle of second-wave feminism – a victory I had once assumed well and won. Exploring the fallout in friendship between two room-mates after one abruptly leaves to get married, *Girlfriends* is a gem of American independent film-making, made at a time when very few women were given opportunities to direct. Much like *Frances Ha*, which stays on its eponymous heroine, *Girlfriends* spends most of its time with Susan (Melanie Mayron), an aspiring photographer living in New York, rather than her married writer friend Annie (Anita Skinner). Susan, with her enchanting Nan Goldin hair and easily stung sensibility, seems hardly to recognise either her friend or herself in the aftermath of their separation. She sits quietly in Annie's new home, uncertain around the sudden, foreign presence of a husband-of-the-house; she is alternately charming and prickly at parties, slipping away from a one-night-stand only to apologise months later. 'I was just coming out of a heavy relationship,' she sheepishly excuses herself. When, in a rare moment of togetherness, Susan and Annie sit looking at photos on a projector, it isn't until moments later that we learn they are not Susan's but snapshots from Annie's honeymoon, given sudden, exhibitive pride of place. Watching Susan's mounting sense of rejection, I am reminded violently of Mira Mattar's novel *Yes, I Am a Destroyer*, and the vignette in which the nameless narrator speaks of her friendships. 'Suddenly it eats at tables,' she writes, 'wedded, and looks askance at the broken, the unhinged, wielding a screwdriver.'[3]

It is the same kind of rupture, the same kind of grief, that Frances experiences – 'you left me,' Susan tells Annie desperately during a fight. But it is a rupture that is also an inquiry into what kind of female life we find legible, or important. Susan and Annie's breakup materialises many of the struggles of second-wave feminism, articulating urgent questions that were being asked at the time (that it seems we are still asking): whether it is possible to engage in heteronormative monogamy and retain the unstructured, queered entanglement of platonic companionship; whether economic and creative freedom are reconcilable with domestic demands; whether it is possible to be truly independent and married. The two women's circumstances are fiercely political precisely in their unexceptional nature: Annie's husband is kind, her baby sweet, Susan's boyfriend irritating in the harmless way so many artsy boys are. There is nothing traumatic or brutally undoing about their situations. They are just inherently limiting.

Annie leaves, and Susan loses not only a partner to do dishes and delightedly make home renovation plans with, but the intimacy that comes from two people both striving for the same thing – untrammelled freedom and creative expression. 'You don't need anyone to take care of you, Annie,' Susan confidently pronounces at the beginning of the film as the two gossip about men, only to tell her now-married friend much later that she no longer knows what is best for her. This new Annie – married, unwriting – is an unknown quantity, a being with desires and needs that Susan cannot peer through the wifely, maternal facade to access. For herself, meanwhile, Susan is certain of what independence signifies. 'I like me when I don't need you,' she tells her boyfriend flatly after an argument.

Yet, perhaps she dismisses her friend too quickly. A room of one's own, a white picket fence: the lives they represent are so wildly apart, yet what they house is so often the same – a woman negotiating impossible circumstances, trying to make her way through the world. Annie is still trying to write, still struggling to carve out her own interiority within the demands of marriage, and Susan recognises this eventually; she returns to Annie, who missed Susan's exhibition opening to recover from an abortion she had in an attempt to cling onto independence. Annie wants to continue her studies, she wants to be married and have children, she wants love and creative fulfilment – a life of wide-open, improbable fullness. The structures that have swallowed her up do not make these desires any less true. *Girlfriends* ends with Susan and Annie sitting childlike on the sofa, throwing sweets into the other's mouth. It is open-ended whether the two will be able to reconcile the diverging pull of their lives; whether marriage and domesticity are, in the end, compatible with such irresponsible intimacy. But it is enough, maybe, to have discovered the want is still there.

Both *Frances Ha* and *Girlfriends* give voice to the complexity of the friendship breakup; they pay attention, and so make it deeply real, and deeply important. The desolation that their suddenly rootless characters experience means that something vital has been lost; a narrative seen in other friendship texts, where contours of intimacy are traced through absence rather than solidity, where blank space is a coda for what has since gone away. Paul Feig's 2011 film *Bridesmaids*, depicting the deteriorating relationship between two best friends after one gets engaged, deploys awkward humour and gross-out comedy to point to a social dysfunctionality, to the sudden gulf that has opened up between the women's inner desires and their external relation. Anna Hope's

2020 novel *Expectations*, about the dwindling, difficult relationship between three university friends as they enter their thirties, flashes between timelines, locating sharp heartache in the immediate contrast between familiarity and unrecognisability. Then there is Jean Chen Ho's 2022 *Fiona and Jane*, a book about friendship in which the friendship barely figures, because it is as much about its missing, memories, aftermaths.

Fiona and Jane is a novel of sorts, although it is really a collection of short stories, all of which are bound together by the eponymous title characters – two Taiwanese-American women living in contemporary America through childhood to middle-age. Like a series of lengthy vignettes, the stories jump back and forth in time and voice, oftentimes focused on either Fiona or Jane living their separate lives; yet the collection is held together by a kind of wistfulness, an ache for a drifted-apart past, that fixes the two women together even across the years and lengths of country that separate them. In adolescence, as is so often the way, the two are dreamily, defiantly inseparable, sharing cars and secrets and that archetypal second-generation sense of alienation. Their relationship begins to seriously drift when the beautiful, promising Fiona moves away to New York City; but the drifting is really catalysed much earlier, when Jane discovers Fiona had kissed their close friend and hadn't told her. The shock of not sharing everything, the quiet, unintended betrayal of holding a piece of oneself separate and close, creates fracture lines in their relationship, points of fragility that are all too primed for collapse.

Life happens, and Fiona and Jane are pulled apart, and so many pages go past in which their friendship is nothing more than a ghostly outline beneath the firm ink of their adulthood. Busied by the sudden tumult of their individual lives – Jane's father commits suicide after a period of estrangement, Fiona looks after an ill friend amidst a string of damaging relationships – their friendship becomes a theoretical familiarity, what Jane calls 'a story... one whose plot I couldn't make sense of.'[4] Both Fiona and Jane are acutely aware of the moniker of best friend – all the history and intimacy and hurt that it holds – and so are reluctant to let it go. Their friendship is, for most of the book, both a talisman of loss and an unbidden declaration of faith – that perhaps the word will find meaning again even after so much time.

It is so easy to lose the thread of someone, but it is also possible to pick it back up; to follow it, Theseus-like, through the labyrinth and back to safety. Much like *Frances Ha* and *Girlfriends*, there is a sense throughout *Fiona and Jane* of things coming apart and then, unbelievably, back together; of feeling like something has been irreparably lost, only to have the tide wash it up, well-worn and bright. It is a breakup narrative where the break never fully holds: Fiona returns to Los Angeles, spent from the heartaches of her twenties, and finds Jane again – the two build separate lives that cautiously, but inevitably, weave the other in. Throughout the book, Fiona and Jane must negotiate what it means to share a life with someone, what it means to access and leave room for another's interiority that is always evolving.

There are times where they resort to silence, where the loneliness both in and apart from each other's company threatens to overwhelm, times where they cannot be a panacea for all of the other's ills. Yet there are also moments where their tentative, oblique faith in their friendship anchors them together, even as their lives drift apart. When Fiona tells Jane that she is pregnant, Jane struggles not to feel a sense of abandonment. 'Fiona was leaving again,' Chen Ho writes. 'She was always leaving. And this time, Jane feared there would be no coming back.'[5] The fear is real – I can feel it so acutely. But there is also the fact – the thing with feathers that cannot die – that Fiona has always, eventually, come back. It is hard to come away from *Fiona and Jane* without the same bruised faith in their unfinished story that propels both women; that has kept them, against the odds, in each other's lives.

I have edged around endings, any kind of ending, all my life. I am frightened of the wreckage they signify, of the ways they can rewrite the happiness of what came before, of what they might say about my ability to withstand hurt. The platonic breakup has always to me sat in abrupt foil to the giddy joys of the friendship text: a kind of harpy warning sign, a sombre oracle of what might happened when our determination to hold fast fails. And while it may well be those things, I am suddenly, guttingly struck by how almost any of the texts that precede this chapter might fit comfortably within it: Issa and Molly's fourth season breakup in *Insecure* that prompted dozens of think pieces about toxic friendships; Lila and Lenù's entire, tense relationship in the Neapolitan novels; the way Laura eventually leaves Tyler for the last time in *Animals*, glancing behind as her friend – drenched in glitter and wine and ecstasy – stands in a bar by herself.

It is heart-breaking, in a way, how such falling apart seems to simply form part of the narrative, just another loss in life that we must accept. But there is also, perhaps, something hopeful in how it suffuses almost every tale of friendship, both real and unreal. Frances and Sophie, Susan and Annie, Fiona and Jane – all three pairs of women figure out a way to return to each other: changed, more sober, but still there. It is what marks the platonic breakup apart from the romantic breakup, a separation that only seems to move in the future tense, that so often demands a rupture from the past. Perhaps, in our friendships, we can find a way back to the relics of who we once were, and who we once loved. Perhaps we might atomise and disperse, but perhaps we might also recollect. I think of every friendship that has felt lost to me, and the magnificent drama of my hurt and abandonment – the panic and shame of being left behind. What if I could accept these friendships as unfinished, rather than lost? What if I could, for once, sit quietly within the end, and see the fading ink disappear down the page, and have faith that there are more pages – unwritten and inviting – still to come?

Conclusion

There is a park on the outskirts of my city: a curious sculpture garden that belongs to another world, that is but a short bus ride away. I first heard about it from a friend several years after having first moved here, and her discovery of it prompted a strange sense of disorientation, as if someone had lifted a flap in a pop-up book to reveal a whole new room to my home that I hadn't known was there. It is a place I have come to associate entirely with my friendships; both because it came to me through her, and because I have since taken so many others there, so that the residues of our intimacies seem to cling to its paths, and I cannot extricate the stories of our lives from its tangled corners.

There is a lot of art in this park, and a lot of magic; and there is one particular work that I seek out every time I am there. Made by Scottish artist Nathan Coley, it is a metal structure with cables running across it like the billboard of an old-fashioned cinema, or the lightly ruled lines that keep an exercise book in check. Letters, traced out in light bulbs and strung between the cables, spell out a fragment of a quote from George Bernard Shaw: YOU IMAGINE WHAT YOU DESIRE. I lean against the edges of the garden the sculpture stands in; I feel the rough knotted wood of the fence against my ribs and hear the echoes of my friends rummaging in a dovecot behind me. I am obsessed with the causality that Coley and Shaw imply, the sense of imbrication: the idea that desire comes first and imagination is what gives it shape, what allows its amorphous, billowing nature to be made visible.

You imagine what you desire. I keep returning to these words, passed down through so many artistic mediations, and I feel so, unbelievably tender towards the eagerness of our imaginations – the desires that they give shape to both in private and public. It was a failure of imagination which concerned Lauren Berlant when they argued for a politics of intimacy beyond heteronormativity: a fear, they explained, that people left on the margins might become unimaginable, even to themselves. In a world where every social, legal, and economic structure demands a singular narrative from us, a singular presentation of our complex selves, it is in the recklessness of our imaginations that new possibilities might become real. New realms of stories spun out, that make bright the depth and fractiousness and abiding attachment of our desires, that offer an understanding of female intimacy away from the structures that have, through all of history, sought to keep it in place.

This book is for all the women and people throughout the centuries who did not have a choice, who were forced into one avenue of intimacy, whose interior lives were only considered legible through the values of the patriarchy and the capitalist state. The women whose friendships were unseen or unacknowledged or not even permitted at all, who felt trapped in the ferocity of desires and dreams of another life that they couldn't articulate. I feel so profoundly haunted by how closely my generation missed such a fate, and by how many in the world continue to live it.

Friendship is not a rote or flimsy thing. It is not a naivety of youth, or an accessory to womanhood, or an emotional crutch, tradable for another, more serious bond. It is tied, rather, to everything that is essential for our survival: sexual liberation and economic freedom and reproductive rights and social security. It is how we might live a life other than the one that has always been laid out before us. It is how we might escape the continued legacies of the patriarchy. It is how we might resist – and rebuild.

Olivia Laing[1] once wrote that loneliness is a city, and I think that is true. But I think, more precisely, that intimacy is a city – populated and unpopulated, haunted and thrumming with life. Its ever-evolving construction – its homes and glades and thoroughfares – lies in our hands, in what we long to give shape to, in who we imagine will walk through its streets. The texts explored in *BFFs* offer such cities in microcosm; they trace brand new blueprints for what the best-friends-forever promise might come to mean, for how we might build out the narratives of our most vital moments. We can follow them from room to room: the frenzy of our coming-of-age attachments, the soft press of another's body and subjectivity on our own, the recalibration of our selfhoods – the joys and the losses of it all. Culture has always been important; it has always allowed us to see what is possible. Here, in the canon of female intimacy, we can see ourselves.

Look around at your life: its complex ecosystems, the lives that have shaped it. The many, many loves that you have had. There is no inevitability to any of it, if we choose for there not to be. Something wonderfully tangled, and fiercely altering, can be imagined, and grasped, and lived and lived.

I take up the old necklaces, knotted together, their jagged edges now so worn. I press the tattered classroom notes, their undecipherable mess of handwritings, down flat. The last school shirt, covered in childish scrawl. The long, long digital archive of correspondence. That one

Tupperware that does not match the others. The already fading polaroids. The immense history of our intimacies, thick everywhere I look.

Maybe forever doesn't have to mean just our own lifetimes. Maybe it stretches beyond.

References

Introduction

1. Christine de Pizan, *The Book of the City of Ladies*. Persea Books, 1998. p. 8.
2. Lauren Berlant, *Intimacy*. University of Chicago Press, 2000. p. 5.
3. Ibid. p. 6.
4. Tom Rasmussen, *First Comes Love: On Marriage and Other Ways of Being Together*. Bloomsbury, 2021. p. 13.
5. Ibid. p. 91.
6. "AITA for putting my single best friends before my married ones all the time?" *Reddit*. 4 February 2020. reddit.com/r/AmItheAsshole/comments/eyqwy8/aita_for_putting_my_single_best_friends_before_my. Accessed 30 December 2022.
7. bell hooks, *All About Love*. HarperCollins, 2001. p. 138.

Chapter 1

1. Nancy K. Miller, *My Brilliant Friends: Our Lives in Feminism*. Columbia University Press, 2019. p. 88.
2. Toni Morrison, *Sula*. Chatto & Windus Ltd, 1980. p. 54-55.
3. Ibid. p. 147.
4. "A Dew-Lined Web: On Sula" Namwali Serpell, *The Paris Review*, 9 February 2022. theparisreview.org/blog/2022/02/09/a-dewlined-web-on-sula. Accessed 30 December 2022.
5. Toni Morrison, *Sula*. Chatto & Windus Ltd, 1980. p. 168.
6. Ibid. p. 119.

7.   Nancy K. Miller, *My Brilliant Friends: Our Lives in Feminism*. Columbia University Press, 2019. p. 84.

8.   "Teaching literature on female friendship in the #MeToo era", Nudrat Kamal, *Prism*, 18 February 2019. dawn.com/news/1464595/teaching-literature-on-female-friendship-in-the-metoo-era. Accessed 30 December 2022.

9.   Jenny Slate, *Little Weirds*. Fleet, 2019. p. 34.

10. Melissa Febos, *Girlhood*. Bloomsbury, 2019. p. 47.

11. Elena Ferrante, *Those Who Leave and Those Who Stay*. Europa Editions, 2014. p. 346-347.

12. George Eliot, *The Mill on the Floss*. W. W. Norton and Company, 1994. p. 36.

Chapter 2

1.   "Notes on Grief" Chimamanda Ngozi Adichie, *The New Yorker*, 10 September 2020. newyorker.com/culture/personal-history/notes-on-grief Accessed 30 December 2022.

2.   Ann Brashares, *The Second Summer of the Sisterhood*. Corgi, 2003. p. 11-12.

3.   Emma Jane Unsworth, *Animals*. Canongate, 2015. p. 97.

4.   Virginie Despentes, *King Kong Theory*. Fitzcarraldo Editions, 2020. p. 25.

5.   "On Finally Watching "Girls," a Different and Better Show Than I'd Been Led To Imagine" Jia Tolentino. *The New Yorker*, 13 April 2017. newyorker.com/culture/jia-tolentino/on-finally-watching-girls-a-different-and-better-show-than-id-been-led-to-imagine. Accessed 30 December 2022.

6.   Jeffrey Eugenides, *The Virgin Suicides*. Bloomsbury, 2011. p. 49.

7.   Ibid. p. 7.

8.   Ibid. p. 246.

9.   Ibid. p. 39.

10. Anna Backman Rogers, *Sofia Coppola: The Politics of Visual Pleasure*. Berghahn Books, 2019. p. 25.

Chapter 3

1. Kayleen Schaefer, *Text Me When You Get Home*. Dutton, 2018. p. 134.
2. Eve Kosofksy Sedgwick, *Tendencies*. Duke University Press, 1993. p. 6.
3. ""I just wanted it to be a regular story about black people": Issa Rae on creating and starring in HBO's Insecure" Caroline Darya Framke, *Vox*, 9 October 2016 vox.com/culture/2016/10/7/13176104/issa-rae-insecure-hbo-interview Accessed 30 December 2022.
4. "The Dance I'm Doing: Crystal Moselle On Skate Kitchen and Betty" Anahit Behrooz, *Girls on Tops*, 10 September 2021 girlsontopstees.com/read-me/2021/9/10/the-dance-im-doing-crystal-moselle-on-skate-kitchen-and-betty Accessed 30 December 2022.
5. Azar Nafisi, *Reading Lolita in Tehran*. Penguin, 2015. p. 58.
6. Ibid. p. 28.

Chapter 4

1. Jenny Odell, *How To Do Nothing: Resisting the Attention Economy*. Melville House Publishing, 2019. p. xxiii.
2. "Frances Ha: The Green Girl" Annie Baker, *Criterion*, 12 November 2013 criterion.com/current/posts/2958-frances-ha-the-green-girl Accessed 30 December 2022.
3. Mira Mattar, *Yes, I Am a Destroyer*. Ma Bibliothèque, 2020. p. 46.
4. Jean Chen Ho, *Fiona and Jane*. Viking, 2022. p. 165.
5. Ibid. p. 232.

Conclusion

1. Olivia Laing, *The Lonely City*. Canongate, 2016. p. 281.

Acknowledgements

First and foremost, the hugeest thank you to Heather McDaid, Laura Jones, and the rest of the team at 404 Ink – for their hard work, for their unwavering support, for believing in this book before it was anything.

I am so grateful to the many editors who have worked with me over the years: especial thanks to Katie Goh, Ella Kemp and David Brake, who all gave me my various starts and without whom I would not be doing any of this. Thank you to *Club des Femmes* and *Extra Teeth* who published what turned out to be early seeds of this book; the fanciest cocktail in the land for the latter's Heather Parry, who advised me on this manuscript and also my taxes (I'm sorry). Thank you also to Nikesh Shukla for a mentoring session that gave so much clarity, and to Sisters Uncut for facilitating it (and for everything else they do).

Enormous thanks to my editor-in-chief at *The Skinny* Rosamund West for letting me skive so many times to write, and to all my other colleagues for picking up so much slack. Shout out also to my Venice and London pals, especially Yasmine Kandil and Anna McKibbin, for life outside of the library.

Most especially, love and thanks to my parents for their eternal support, and to my siblings for their eternal enthusiasm. A particularly huge thank you to my older brother Arash Behrooz, for making the conditions of writing this book possible.

And finally. To Helen Austin, Eleanor Bally, Helen Brooks, Cami Bullins, Rho Chung, Charlotte Diffey, Amy Elizabeth, Katie Goh (twice, baby!), Katie Hawthorne, Anneke Hoffmann, Niki Holzapfel, Harriet MacMillan, Christina Neuwirth, Robyn Pritzker, Tabussum Rasheed, Hannah Schmidt, Xuanlin Tham and, of course, the lights of my life Bridget Moynihan and Maria Torres-Quevedo. This book is from you, for you, and about you. Thank you for making my world so big.

About the Author

Photo: Ella Kemp

Anahit Behrooz is a writer, editor and critic based in Edinburgh. She works as Books Editor and Events Editor at *The Skinny*, and writes for *AnOther Magazine*, *Little White Lies*, *gal-dem* and *Girls on Tops* among others.

About the Inklings series

This book is part of 404 Ink's Inkling series which presents big ideas in pocket-sized books.

They are all available at 404ink.com/shop.

If you enjoyed this book, you may also enjoy these titles in the series:

Whatever Next?: On Adult Adoptee Identities

Inspired by the conversations within their Whatever Next? community project, Jo, Addie and Hannah explore the key tropes that adoptees grapple with and how these conversations are evolving, with the goal of kickstarting new dialogues around the adoption experience more broadly, and showcase how beneficial shared discussion can be.

The End: Surviving the World Through Imagined Disasters – Katie Goh

The End studies apocalypse fiction and its role in how we manage, manifest and imagine social, economic and political disaster and crises. What do apocalypse narratives tell us about how we imagine our place in history? Why do we fantasise about the end of the world? What does this all unveil about our contemporary anxieties?

No Man's Land: Living Between Two Cultures – Anne East

In *No Man's Land*, Anne East explores the chasm of living between two cultures, how it is to feel one thing and yet be perceived as another, the emotions felt within this limbo, and why culture truly matters. More so, she considers how this has manifested through history, and the British Empire, with focus on the often unheard or ignored impacts on those of East and Southeast Asian heritage.